The Communist and Social systems have always had support from some philosoph now. Michael Novak's bo which form the bedrock of democratic capitalism. To he adds those of a philoso the case for a way of life rapidly spreading around the globe.

—WALTER B. WRISTON
Former Chairman,
Citicorp/Citibank

An easy-to-read and practical book on the subject of business as a vocation for those interested in the interactions between political and economic systems and their borders with theological thought.

—ROBERTO C. GOIZUETA
Chairman of the Board and CEO
The Coca-Cola Company

If the service is beneficial, then every useful work is a calling and a blessing for all people. Michael Novak clearly explains in this scholarly book that by free competition, business and science have multiplied the standard of living about 100-fold in only 200 years, and thereby prove beneficial just as the Christian ministry is beneficial.

—SIR JOHN M. TEMPLETON
Donor of the Templeton Prizes
for Progress in Religion

Capitalists with no conscience are a problem; capitalists with a bad conscience are a bigger problem. The purpose of this splendid book is not to put a moral gloss on grubby business, but to demonstrate the moral excitement of business itself. Business leaders who accept Novak's challenge should be prepared to be changed—in how they think, how they work, how they live, and how they give. I have no doubt they will be grateful for the change on all scores.

—RICHARD JOHN NEUHAUS
Editor in Chief, *First Things*

OTHER BOOKS BY MICHAEL NOVAK

Choosing Presidents
The Experience of Nothingness
The Spirit of Democratic Capitalism
Free Persons and the Common Good
This Hemisphere of Liberty
Ascent of the Mountain, Flight of the Dove
The Catholic Ethic and the Spirit of Capitalism
Toward a Theology of the Corporation
The New Consensus on Family and Welfare (Editor)
The Guns of Lattimer
Belief and Unbelief
The Open Church
The Joy of Sports
Unmeltable Ethnics

FICTION
The Tiber Was Silver
Naked I Leave

BUSINESS
AS A CALLING

Work and the Examined Life

Michael Novak

THE FREE PRESS

THE FREE PRESS
A Division of Simon & Schuster Inc.
1230 Avenue of the Americas
New York, NY 10020

THE FREE PRESS and colophon are trademarks
of Simon & Schuster Inc.

Designed by REM Studio, Inc.

Manufactured in the United States of America

11 13 15 17 19 20 18 16 14 12

Library of Congress Cataloging-in-Publication Data

Novak, Michael.
    Business as a calling: work and the examined life/Michael
Novak.
        p.   cm.
    Includes bibliographical references and index.
    ISBN 0-684-82748-4
    1. Work ethic.   I. Title.
HD4905.N65   1996
306.3'6—dc20   96-482
                                                CIP

ISBN: 978-1-4767-4572-5

To my sister, Mary Ann Novak,
vice president of Parsons, Brinckerhoff,
whose vocation is business.
She is also the best sister
four older brothers
ever had.

and

In homage to Pope John Paul II

Contents

✛

Introduction

✧

PLENTY ISN'T ENOUGH

What doth it profit a man if he gain the whole world and
suffer the loss of his soul?

—Mark 8:36

This inquiry is for Jews, Christians, Muslims and others who
take the inner life seriously, including those who while hesitant
to belong to any church take seriously their vocation as
thoughtful and self-questioning beings.

Those who have eaten awhile of material success know that
there is more to life than bread. They desire more than *having*.

Many are haunted by the awareness that they are not getting all that is to be drunk of life, that (as Thomas Wolfe suggested in *Look Homeward, Angel*) there is somewhere *an
unfound door*, through which what they seek is revealed, up

ahead. The most hardheaded people often feel this most keenly. Whatever they attain, that isn't it—not what they are looking for.

Many who read these pages may be unsure what it is that calls them. All they know is that their hearts are restless. They are happy in what they do, but they somehow know, by a kind of inner intimation, that they could do better what they do, if someone could help them grasp the larger picture, and focus on what they really want to do with their lives. On what they ought to do, to heed the inner calling.

Or, perhaps, not exactly on what they *ought* to do. Rather, on what they are invited to do, could do, would find more beautiful to do, would certainly attract them to do—if only they knew what it is.

Further, I imagine that such potential readers are numerous, that there is tremendous, untapped good will in them, and that everything I am about to write is in some sense already known to them, not perhaps in a way that they can put into words, but in a way that will ring true to them the minute they hear it said.

When a philosopher, or theologian, is doing his work well, he is only putting into words what already is obscurely known to those who share with him the same human nature, the same destiny. There is a difference, St. Thomas Aquinas once wrote, between the experiential knowledge that a chaste man has of chastity, even if never articulated, and the abstract, theoretical knowledge of the concept of chastity that a theologian has. There is a "knowledge by connaturality," a knowledge that comes by alert living, doing, striving, and receiving, even when this knowledge is never put into words, but left in a kind of verbal darkness.

This tacit knowledge, based upon experience, differs from the knowledge that comes from books, which allows one to make many learned distinctions and to articulate various subtle points. (One and the same person, of course, may have both kinds of knowledge.)

Both kinds of knowledge are good. Yet knowledge by connaturality is, in a sense, more fundamental than book knowledge. It is the real, existent ground that allows book knowledge, or at least some book knowledge, to "ring true," and to become assimilated into one's daily living. I am going to count heavily in what follows on what many already know tacitly, but have never had a chance to see confirmed in the words of others.

There is gain in seeing such things in words, in learning to make distinctions and connections, and in seeing one's basic convictions set out in a more or less systematic way. First of all, to the extent that they are confirmatory, such words help one to do even better what one had been doing, with a greater clarity and concentration. To the extent that they are challenging, or even merely stretching, such words help one to think more clearly about one's actions and perhaps even to enlarge their scope and to improve their execution.

Not many years ago, a friend of mine who had grown up in Gary, Indiana, went home to visit some old high school buddies, one of whom was the owner and manager of an old family factory that was being forced to lay off a couple score of workers.

In his office, stony faced, the manager explained to his old friend why this was sad but necessary, the pressures he was under, the bottom line, what was happening all around the country in the machine parts business he was in. There is no alternative, he said, plunging his pudgy fist into his open hand. It's tough, but that's business. My friend was sympathetic, even admired the kind of asceticism the manager had to live under, and found himself wondering whether he, a journalist, often a freelancer, would be able to summon up the discipline to fire almost 50 people.

Then, afterwards, to talk about old times, the two of them retired to a neighborhood bar. Over beers, the manager started going over the same ground, the firings. His whole mode of speech changed. He began reciting names, and telling when they had begun to work with him, who had kids in college, whose wives were sick, how uncomprehending most of them were about what they would do next. Before long, tears were coming down his face.

It was as though he had to live two lives, one as a professional, the owner and manager, who could talk tough about the bottom line, the other as an old buddy talking about what was now bothering him. The two quite different languages coming from the same man was what most struck my friend. Not as though one were a private language, a language of the sentiments, and the other a professional language, the language of necessity, although that was certainly a part of the picture. Rather, a strictly economic, business language has grown up without including within itself the moral, religious, even humane language appropriate to its own activities.

The virtual monopoly on ways of thinking about business life exercised by economics as a science and the business schools as schools of hardnosed practicality has had an unfortunate effect upon the moral and religious dimension of economic life. It has tended to focus exclusive attention on material things, on the bottom line, on instrumental matters, on means and methods, rather than on ends and purposes. Among other things my hope for this book and volumes like it is that they will gradually change the way business schools talk about people in business.

For various historical reasons, economics and business faculties have often pictured their disciplines as more like the sciences, or more like the *servile* and *useful* arts, than like the liberal arts.

They have been complacently concerned almost exclusively

with *means* rather than with *ends*—which, often enough, they have been quite content to leave to ministers, bishops, confessors, moralists, and other (as they see things) more woolly headed thinkers. "We'll tell you *how* to get there, the costs and the benefits, but as for the ends, goals, purposes, values, that's up to you. Talk to your chaplain." We all know where that leaves the chaplain.

Worse still, experience teaches, religious leaders speak inadequately about business—more so than about almost anything else they preach on. Their professional vocabulary, for the most part, so misses the point that it is painful to listen to them. Some of them, of course, have been misled by the kind of leftist sentiments uttered by the great Harvard theologian, Paul Tillich, who wrote, long before the collapse of socialism in 1989: "Any serious Christian must be a socialist."

Others of them speak of economic behavior in an ancient aristocratic language, looking down on "vulgar mammon." The clergy, in the manners and methods of their education, belong historically to the aristocratic traditions of the liberal arts.

BORED WITH MAKING MONEY

Those whose religious and moral vocation in life is played out in one of the many fields of business get little enough help, then, from those they would normally turn to for instruction. Sometimes in sermons, pastoral letters, and other manifestoes of their churches, they get the impression that religious leaders don't object to wealth if it is inherited; in fact, they rather count upon the largesse of established families of "old" money. But if you actually made the money yourself, in your own lifetime, maybe starting from nothing, you are given the subtle impression that that, by contrast, is rather sweaty, vulgar, and morally suspect. The making of money is taken to be a sign of "materialism."

Some people, alas, *are* driven mainly by materialism. One does meet people, not many of them in my experience, who live for nothing else but making money, and who seem to be satisfied, for a time at least, by the showy "good life" that having money permits. Those who believe that that option is often taken, however, must ask themselves if they really believe that "Man does not live by bread alone." The truth is that man does not.

Most human beings cannot stand the effort to live a purely materialistic life, not for long at least. One meets a lot of people of middling age, bored with making money and the mundane disciplines that effort imposes on them. One meets even more who, after an immersion in the disciplines of their profession and the enjoyment (often rushed and harried) of its rewards, find themselves saying even aloud: "There's got to be more than this." Some begin looking to public service, or to philanthropy, or to civic work to put more "meaning" into their lives.

The French philosopher Jacques Maritain, one of the architects of the Universal Declaration of Human Rights, once observed that a great deal of religious rhetoric warning against riches, materialism, and worldly pleasures is based on the assumptions of an age of scarcity—and on the suspicion that such things might actually be fulfilling. He predicted (this was in 1944) that as affluence began to grow again in America and elsewhere after the war, the psychology of wealth and the enjoyment of material plenty would turn out quite otherwise. The aftertaste of affluence is boredom.

Maritain was quite certain that man does not live by bread alone. When men began to have enough bread as a matter of course, an abundance of bread, he predicted, material appetites would lose their edge. Humans would become interested in larger and more satisfying horizons—in the things of the spirit, for which their hungers are infinite and in no danger of being sated, in prayer and contemplation, in the arts, in philanthropy, and in general in improving the lot of their fellow human beings. There, he thought, lie far more satisfying aspirations.

People in the field of religion, he warned, would need to develop an entirely new form of apologetic and spiritual counselling. In this judgment, I am certain that Maritain was correct. Such prescience arose because his spirit was unusually pure, open to the better angels of our nature, and without envy. (A professor of mine at Harvard, a happy atheist, once told me that Maritain, when he taught there, impressed him as the only saint he had ever met.)

THE ANTI-BUSINESS SKEPTICS

When strangers and acquaintances asked me about the subject of this book, I more than once encountered incredulity. Business as a calling? People in business, religious? Businesspeople, moral?

Many persons educated in the humanities (with their aristocratic traditions) and the social sciences (with their quantifying, collectivist traditions) are uncritically anticapitalist. They think of business as vulgar, philistine, and morally suspect.

The most unthinking in this regard, as Michael Medved shows in *Hollywood vs. America*, are the post-1960s Hollywood filmmakers. Prior to 1965, television shows portrayed businessmen as good guys twice as often as bad guys. In the 1970s, this ratio was reversed—two villains for every good guy.

Today, big business has become television's favorite villain. Medved quotes an exhaustive analysis of prime time television by the sociologists Richter, Richter and Rothman which concludes: "*By 1980 a majority of the CEO's portrayed on prime time committed felonies.*" Respectable businessmen were by then committing 40 percent of the murders on prime time television, and 44 percent of vice crimes like drug trafficking and pimping.

All this is far removed from Hollywood's Golden Age in

the '30s and '40s, when in George Cukor's classic, *Dinner at Eight*, Lionel Barrymore played a dignified shipping magnate, and in the all-time favorite *It's a Wonderful Life*, Jimmy Stewart played a humane, compassionate, and (believe this or not) *likable* banker.

So it is easy these days, even against the prompting of common sense, to think flabbily about business—to let pass without resistance repeated images that a life spent in business is probably immoral or criminal.

In actual fact, we usually expect people in business, especially in the large corporations, to be buttoned-down and traditional in their moral lives—far from being fans of permissiveness or promoters of the "new morality." Beyond the Hollywood pretense that people in business are morally derelict, the other criticism most often heard from artistic and academic types is that they lead morally *boring* lives. Which is it?

When they heard I was doing this book, three accusations came up among strangers and friends. The first was based on such matters as Benetton and Calvin Klein ads and Time Warner's brutal, worse-than-pornographic "gangsta rap." It was usually phrased this way: In pursuit of profits, won't businesses act immorally whenever necessary?

The second typical accusation was as follows: Aren't executive salaries out of line? Isn't dramatic inequality wrong?

The third accusation deplored downsizing: Isn't it wrong to subject workers and middle managers in their mature years to so much insecurity? Isn't it wrong to let people go abruptly and without a parachute?

My general position on these three questions has two parts. First, business is a morally serious enterprise, in which it is possible to act either immorally or morally. Second, by its own internal logic and inherent moral drive, business *requires* moral conduct; and, not always, but with high probability, violations of this logic lead to personal and business disgrace.

In the examples mentioned above, both Calvin Klein and Time Warner backed down, precisely because they saw harm being done to their businesses. Deviations from the public moral code invite retribution. In Time Warner's case, there are indications that even personal shame was involved. When William Bennett and Delores Tucker asked the top officers of the corporation, around a table, to read aloud the lyrics of the rap songs in question, the officers refused to do so. Mr. Bennett also urged them, to their obvious discomfiture, to read these lyrics aloud to their own children.

To return to the general point: It *is* possible for people in business to do moral wrong, even though such wrongdoing sooner or later injures both the business in question and the moral reputation of the profession as a whole. Immoral acts do occur in business. But to behave immorally is neither necessary to nor conducive to business success. One may get away with immoral behavior for a while, but sooner or later it is highly likely to catch up with the perpetrator *and* the firm.

A significant range of immoral behavior in business has been banned by law; business is a highly regulated field of activity. But some things that are not illegal are immoral. Individuals in a religiously and morally pluralistic society may differ on where such moral lines should be drawn, and in a morally confused age such as our own this line may be more blurry than usual. But no one can deny there *are* morally impassable lines. (Even our literary nihilists tend to promote this nihilism as a *moral* position: more "honest," more "brave," etc.)

Virtually everyone would be embarrassed to have splashed across the front pages of major newspapers every wrong they ever did. Accordingly, more than one business leader has announced to his workforce: "Anything you would be ashamed to see in the newspapers, just don't do." Joe Calihan of Bradford Partners in Pittsburgh puts it another way: "A dollar made dishonestly is not a dollar this firm wants to make." His firm's moral reputation is an asset it cannot afford to lose.

Moreover, no matter what the newspapers or the public might find immoral, there are still certain things of which some corporate executives will say: "No matter what anybody else does, there are certain things this firm will never do. Do them and you're out." High moral standards of this sort sometimes turn out to be, especially over time, a competitive advantage. True enough, high moral standards incur costs; some contracts may well be lost. As in other walks of life, moral fidelity is never cost-free. Yet far from being an impediment to success in business, moral conduct is in the long run more in keeping with probabilities of success than is immoral behavior. People can scarcely help preferring to do business with honest and morally trustworthy associates, rather than with liars, scoundrels, and moral weaklings.

THREE SPECIFIC OBJECTIONS

To return to the three specific questions raised above:

1. Yes, some people in business do have lax moral standards, and others think that the sole driving force in business (and the only morally legitimating one) is making profits. Still others occasionally, even if not often, are guilty of moral lapses. Business is a morally serious enterprise, however, and persons of suspect moral character cannot and will not escape moral judgment, sometimes from their own consciences, sometimes by the moral disapprobation (private or public) of others, and in the end by the Judge of all of us. That there is such a Judge (or at least a transpersonal standard) we all testify when we exclaim that certain actions—even if they go unpunished by law and public opinion—morally *stink*.

An indication that such a moral dynamism is at work, even among some who violate it, is that business practices, over the generations, keep being held to higher standards. Some things done without shame in the nineteenth century are today regarded by business leaders as morally primitive and impermissible. Thus, even if individuals (or an entire generation) are for some time blind to them, moral standards slowly make their presence felt, sometimes by way of shocking abuses that stir the public. (Of course, over time moral standards may *decline*, too, thus setting the stage in a later era for a moral reawakening. Our own era seems to be at the beginning of such a reawakening.)

2. There are two sound responses to the question of stratospheric executive compensation. The first is that the most destructive passion in any free society is envy (see chapters four and seven). Anything that incites envy—or seems to support the arguments of those moved by envy—is a danger to the free society. Even the *appearance* of excessive compensation, seemingly far beyond the bounds of common sense, injures both democracy and capitalism.

With James Madison, I hold that the passion for absolute equality is wicked and self-destructive. Except in terms of equal standing under the rule of law, equality is not a morally acceptable social ideal. Yet, observation shows that business executives are blind to the social destructiveness of current levels of compensation. Current practices give the appearance of cozy collusion, in which executives on one another's governing boards scratch one another's backs, heedless of the sacrifices others in their firms are making. For the sake of the moral reputation of business, executive belt-tightening is desperately needed, and moral leadership from somewhere in business must step forward. If the whole country is tightening its belt, to be morally credible business leaders must also be seen to do so.

The second argument does not invalidate the first but sets it in context. The extraordinary skills required to manage a large modern firm are extremely rare, and the competition to attract top talent pushes their market value to unprecedented heights. Finding just the right top talent may be worth scores of millions of dollars to a large corporation. A single inspired business decision by the right chief executive officer is likely to mean far more to a firm's future earnings than his total earnings over the five or so years that he is likely to be at the helm (the average service of a chief executive officer is about that of a professional football player).

The skills required by a business executive today are many, varied, and not often found in combination. Among them are the ability to grasp the possibilities of new technologies, to understand complex market forces, to master financial questions complicated by instantaneous international transactions, and to provide moral and intellectual leadership for a large (and often widely dispersed) corporation, while attending to crucial matters of personnel.

When I asked him about this, one of the leading talent-searchers ("headhunters") for top executives for major firms, Gerard R. Roche (Heidrick and Struggles, Inc., New York), told me that "Everyone wants a Jack Welch, but there's only one Jack Welch, and not many of his caliber. The truly great talent is extremely rare." There are too many buyers chasing too few great talents; no wonder the market price goes up. "Everyone wants a great operating officer, who is also great on vision and strategic change," Roche says. "There are few enough who are great on one of these counts, but on two? Not enough to fill the demand out there."

Moreover, except for the inventors of new technologies or new business concepts who are also owners of their company's original stock (such as Bill Gates of Microsoft and Sam Walton of Walmart), most business leaders are likely to be paid less well than stars of the entertainment industry such as Oprah Winfrey, Michael Jordan, Robert Redford, and Bill Cosby. If a market test is considered fair for entertainers, why is it unfair for creators of new wealth through business? My answer is that it may not be unfair, but that for the first reason mentioned above it may destroy moral esteem for the business system. How to give away great wealth is, furthermore, a serious and unavoidable moral question.

3. One of the structural and inherent moral weaknesses of capitalism as a system is that the creativity, inventiveness, and questioning spirit that make it dynamic have a moral downside and impose a heavy human cost, sometimes even on top executives and investors. The great economist Joseph Schumpeter called this characteristic of the system "creative destruction." Many new technologies make old technologies—and the industries and firms based upon them—obsolete. In addition, firms not living up to their wealth-creating potential are subject to being bought out by value-seekers, who see ways to turn existing assets to better economic use. In both cases, many persons are subject to losing their jobs—sometimes from the top of the firm to the bottom, but most often at levels below the top. Many personal tragedies may result.

This is not a morally commendable aspect of capitalism. Its best defense is that the known alternatives are worse.

A GLANCE AHEAD

A career in business is not only a morally serious vocation but a morally noble one. Those who are called to it have reason to take pride in it and to rejoice in it.

But what is a "calling"? The great sociologist Max Weber wrote of "Politics as a Vocation," and so "Business as a Vocation" was my first working title for this book. "Calling," however, seemed the more common word in English. The best way to grasp the concrete meaning of these synonyms, in any case, is through examples.

The method I will follow is different from most. The artists of Slovakia, the land of my grandparents, were among the world's most loving woodcarvers; the Church of Sv. Pavel in Levoca is one of the wonders of European folk art. When a woodcarver picks up a piece of wood, he studies first its own contours, feels out its own substance and shape and tendencies and grains. He knows that he must work with what is natural to it, with the laws and possibilities of its own being.

Ethicists should always do the same. Inherent in the practices of any profession are its own laws and possibilities. One ought to study the ideals inherent in those before imposing anything else upon them. It is true enough that one will have to cut and carve, and bring out a new and distinctive shape. Yet it is quite necessary to go with the grain—unless one decides that the whole project is useless, and throws aside the worthless stick.

In this spirit, I want to look first at business—at commerce, at industry—to see what ideals are inherent within it. I want to gauge its possibilities, especially its moral and religious possibilities. I want to see what is possible within it, before attempting to lead it to still higher aims. This is a good practice. The first law of ethical reflection is to listen, and only then to guide.

Throughout this book, I draw upon examples from real life, but especially at the beginning it seems useful to recount the stories of men and women who teach us about the business calling by trying to live it out. They may not always do so successfully, or to the satisfaction of their consciences and aspirations, but they learn even by failing.

Business is a demanding vocation, and one is not good at it just by being in it, or even by making piles of money. The bottom line of a calling is measured by pain, learning, and grace. Having a good year in financial terms is hard enough; having a good year in fulfilling one's calling means passing tests that are a lot more rewarding. The difference is a little like being drafted into the army and, instead, volunteering for the green berets.

Doing anything as a calling—especially doing something quite difficult—is a lot more fulfilling than merely drifting.

For this reason, I begin by listening to other voices telling us about their callings. (I would be glad to hear from readers who wish to tell their stories, too.)

But I want to listen, as well, to the rhythms inherent in business as a set of distinctive social practices. And to the even longer waves and rhythms inherent in the sort of worldwide system—the capitalist economy in a democratic culture—in which today business flourishes.

For half of the pleasure from the business calling derives from a sense that the system of which it is a part is highly beneficial to the human race, morally sound, and one of the great social achievements of all time. The other half is personal—finding purpose and meaning in what one does.

That this system is yet unfinished, and has many faults, is one of its attractive challenges: There is much to be done to improve it.

Let us begin by listening to voices from the world of work.

Chapter One

✿

WHAT IS A CALLING?

Vocation (Lat. *vocatio*, a calling): the function or career toward which one believes himself to be called.
——*New World Dictionary, 2d college ed.*

The earning of money within the modern economic order is, so long as it is done legally, the result and the expression of virtue and proficiency in a calling. . . . And in truth this peculiar idea, so familiar to us today, but in reality so little a matter of course, of one's duty in a calling, is what is most characteristic of the social ethic of capitalist culture, and is in a sense the fundamental basis of it . . . Now it is unmistakable that even in the German word *Beruf*, and perhaps still more clearly in the English *calling*, a religious conception, that of a task set by God, is at least suggested.
——*Max Weber*

There is something about business no one may have told you in business school or economics class. Something important.

Maybe more important than anything else in your life, except your marriage and your children.

It is the answer to this question: During their busy lives, what gives people in business their greatest pleasure, and what at the end of their lives gives them their greatest satisfaction?

Whatever it is, don't we often call this "fulfillment"? But fulfillment of *what*? Not exactly a standing order that we placed ourselves. We didn't give ourselves the personalities, talents, or longings we were born with. When we fulfill these— these gifts from beyond ourselves—it is like fulfilling something we were meant to do. It is a sense of having uncovered our personal destiny, a sense of having been able to contribute something worthwhile to the common public life, something that would not have been there without us—and, more than that, something that we were good at and something we enjoyed.

Even if we do not always think of it that way, each of us was given a calling—by fate, by chance, by destiny, by God. Those who are lucky have found it.

CALLINGS

But what exactly is a calling—or (for those who insist) an identity? How would we know one if we saw it? What do you look for, if you wish to find your own?

One good way is to mull over examples from the lives of others. First, though, we need to understand that in our culture (vast and many-faceted as it is), we expect each calling (each personal identity) to be unique. No two people have exactly the same calling. That is why we need to mull over many examples if we are trying to apply them to ourselves. None will ever quite fit; some may suggest useful clues, and some may leave us cold.

Here are several stories of callings I've encountered over the years, including one about myself. Limited pretty much to the field of business, they should give a larger sense of what it means to heed a calling.

↯ M. Scott Peck, M.D., the famous author, tells the story of a young enlisted man in Okinawa who served under him as a practicing therapist. Peter was unusually good at his assignment, and Dr. Peck tried to get him to enter graduate school on his return to the United States. "You're a fine therapist. I could help you get into a good master's program. Your GI Bill would pay for it."

The young soldier said he wanted to start a business. Dr. Peck admits to being "aghast."

As Dr. Peck began reciting the advantages of a career in psychotherapy, he was stopped cold by the young enlisted man: "Look, Scotty, can't you get it in your head that not everyone is like you?" Not every one wants to be a psychotherapist.

Callings are like that. To identify them, two things are normally required: the God-given ability to do the job, and (equally God-given) enjoyment in doing it because of your desire to do it.

↯ In my case, I studied for the Catholic priesthood for twelve and a half years, at the end of which (after a long, dark struggle) I came to know clearly that the priesthood was not my calling. I abandoned my studies five months before ordination. I enjoyed every minute of those twelve-plus years and am everlastingly grateful for them. I loved my friends and colleagues and had many great priests around as models (plus one or two likeable odd ones, who for my generation of students provided a treasure house of anecdotes). I had the advantages of superb spiritual direction and, toward the end, an outside psychotherapist to help me sort things out. Himself a silent Sphinx, he made me sort it out myself. In the end, though, the answer came most clearly during months of silent prayer.

Callings are sometimes like that.

I not only felt much inner resistance to the priesthood—insisting that this was not my vocation—but also an inner drive of my being toward becoming a writer, being involved in politics and social change, trying my hand at fiction, exploring new territories in philosophy and theology. All of these ventures would involve me, I knew, in controversy. It would be enough to defend myself, it seemed, without implicating the whole church (as were I a priest, I would). I needed to be a bit more of a Lone Ranger than a priest ought to be.

↓ John Templeton, founder of the Templeton Growth Fund and perhaps the greatest investor of our time, whom in recent years I have come to know and admire tremendously, told *Forbes* magazine recently that when he was young, he had wanted to become a missionary. From his early days in Winchester, Tennessee, and continuing through his years at Yale and then at Oxford as a Rhodes scholar, he had been a devout young man. At Yale and Oxford, he met a number of Christian missionaries home from abroad and recognized, finally, that he didn't have that kind of stuff.

"I realized that they had more talent as missionaries than I did," he remembers. "But I also realized that I was more talented with money than they were. So I decided to devote myself to helping the missionaries financially." In fact, Sir John (he was knighted by Queen Elizabeth in 1987 for his wide-ranging accomplishments) pioneered in the field of international investing, typically being the first to invest where things looked bleakest and showing extraordinary patience.

His financial success has been amazing. So also has been his worldwide philanthropy. In retirement, he is carrying his philanthropy to new areas—chiefly those concerned with ideas and the formation of the virtue and character necessary for human freedom.

Incidentally, to this day, he flies tourist class, preferring to invest the savings he retains.

One can see in Sir John's several books that he has drawn great drafts of objectivity, perspective, patience, and calm judgment from time devoted every day to prayer. He treats his lifetime occupation, global investing, as a calling God made him to do his best at.

↓ Edward Crosby Johnson II, another talented investor, is best known for starting Fidelity Investments, today the largest mutual fund company in the country. Known in investment circles as "Mister Johnson," he was the grandson of both a doctor and a missionary. Mister Johnson's father, Samuel Johnson, followed neither the medical nor the ministerial route. Instead, he was drafted into a family retailing business, which he never enjoyed. What really interested Samuel were his hobbies, including the study of pre-Christian religions.

Mister Johnson inherited his father's interest in religion, especially Eastern religious philosophies, because they gave him another way of looking at the world and understanding people. But it was his father's lack of enthusiasm for his work—compared to the passion he had for his hobbies—that convinced Mister Johnson early on that he wanted to do something he was good at and enjoyed. Initially, he chose law as a profession, but he soon discovered law wasn't his calling. Investing (and the psychology of the stock market) was. To him, the stock market was "like a beautiful woman, endlessly fascinating, endlessly complex, always changing, always mystifying."

In 1943, he decided to turn his hobby into a full-time career by buying the management contract for (or the right to manage) a small Boston-based mutual fund, Fidelity Fund. Thus, Fidelity Investments began by one man's pursuing his natural interests. In the 1940s, mutual funds—separate legal entities that pooled the money of many small investors—were still catching on. What they offered individuals was diversification and professional management at a reasonable cost—something previously available only to the wealthy.

Providing a service that had never before been readily available delighted Mister Johnson. He wrote to his Harvard classmates in 1945: "It is a real thrill to try to give the small investor—of which our companies are mainly comprised—as good a job of investing as the big man gets." That thought nourished him throughout his life as he increased the range of funds available to small investors.

⋆ Kenneth Lay, chairman and chief executive officer of the largest natural gas company in the United States (and one of the largest in the world), Enron Corp of Houston, some time ago announced publicly his company's vision: "To become the first natural gas major . . . the most innovating and reliable provider of clean energy worldwide." His greatest inward satisfaction, however, has a somewhat different focus.

"In my own case," Lay confided, "I grew up the son of a Baptist minister. From this background, I was fully exposed to not only legal behavior but moral and ethical behavior and what that means from the standpoint of leading organizations and people. I was, and am, a strong believer that one of the most satisfying things in life is to create a highly moral and ethical environment in which every individual is allowed and encouraged to realize their God-given potential. There are few things more satisfying than to see individuals reach levels of performance that they would have thought was virtually impossible for themselves."

⋆ Lorraine Miller spent two years as a VISTA volunteer in

North Carolina, and a career in business was the furthest thing from her mind. At that time, she thought that "creating a profit also created poverty." After winning the Utah Small Business Person of the Year Award, she won the same award for the entire United States in 1994. She didn't get started in business because she wanted to make money; because her first boss had offended her, she wanted to be her own boss (incidentally, one of the three most frequently cited motives among small businessmen). Back in Utah she had noticed that neither outdoor nurseries nor florists supplied the market with potted house plants and decided to spend half her $2,000 in savings on a small stock of such plants in a store she named the Glass Menagerie. Every weekend she drove twelve hours each way to California in her VW van in search of unusual plants. "When you're 25 years old, you can work all day and drive all night, and still have plenty of energy," she told *Nation's Business*. For the first five years, her income was below the poverty line, and she knew nothing about filing regular government reports mandated by labor laws, since as a self-employed person she didn't have to know.

About five years after her start-up, she moved into a new store under a new name, Cactus & Tropicals, hired her first employee, built a greenhouse, and began selling wholesale to grocery chains. She learned quickly enough that margins are higher in retail and went back to that, while starting an ambitious new program on the side: taking care of plants (now 2 million of them) on maintenance contract for commercial establishments. She was then employing thirty-five persons. She still wasn't in it for the money.

When she was told, on receiving her national and statewide awards, that she had "peaked," she got energized. She began planning to increase her business from $1 million to $5 million in sales within three years. Now she was in it for the money: "I want to create a space where my employees can grow, too, and to do that for them—helping them with their educations and things like that—I have to make a lot of money."

You can pay yourself poverty wages at the beginning, but you can't find and keep good workers except by paying good wages and benefits. Making more money didn't make her life easier, of course. She went into business to be her own boss; now her business is her boss, and it's a demanding one at that. But this business is hers.

↓ Building a corporate community of a certain type was also the deepest satisfaction of the business career of Robert Malott, retired chairman of the FMC Corporation in Chicago. At his retirement, he was lauded for a number of highly significant achievements in the firm. "One can be thanked," he later noted, "for successful events, but to be recognized for establishing a 'corporate culture' about which one can be proud, is much more significant." This satisfaction was driven home to him by a manager of his whom he had lauded at a retirement party a little earlier than his own. The insight arrived via a handwritten note:

> Bob, thanks so much for your kind words at my retirement party. The praise and credit you granted me was quite thoughtful and much appreciated. It has been a privilege to be associated with you for the past 20 years. The high standards of performance you set, coupled with your spotless integrity, made me better than I might otherwise have been. Although you graciously gave me credit for many things, it was only your leadership, guidance and unrelenting demand to do the best possible job that allowed me to do what I did. It is a truism that the character of an organization reflects the character of the person at the top, and all credit goes to you for making FMC truly great over the years you were at the helm. It was a wonderful journey; thanks so much for all your help along the way.

Bob Malott cherishes that letter as much as the memory of any other business achievement. Some men are born leaders and get their greatest pleasure from the *esprit de corps* they can build up, in the task-driven enterprise that a business is. That, too, is a kind of calling.

↓ A quite different angle is taken by David Packard of Hewlett-Packard, who got his start in a garage in Palo Alto. Packard's public language is typically quite secular, as when he discussed why a company exists in the first place: "Why are we here? I think many people assume, wrongly, that a company exists solely to make money." Packard knows that making money is an important result of a company's existence, if the company is any good. But a result isn't a cause. "We have to go deeper and find the real reasons for our being. As we investigate this, we inevitably come to the conclusion that a group of people get together and exist as an institution that we call a company so that they are able to accomplish something collectively that they could not accomplish separately—they make a contribution to society, a phrase which sounds trite but is fundamental."

Part of the business vocation, then, is getting together and forming a task-oriented community—a community, in other words, not to satisfy all needs but to get a few specific things done—done for the public, "to make a contribution to society" that no one person could make alone but must be made by many together. Most business callings are not for loners, although for them there are some niche businesses and many niches within most business firms. On the whole, a certain instinct for community and working well with others is highly desirable, if not required. Good social habits—and even social graces—are significant assets.

But Packard's point is deeper than this. "You can look around and still see underlying drives" at work in businesses.

These come "largely from a desire to do something else—to make a product—to give a service—generally, to do something which is of value." "The real reason for Hewlett-Packard's existence is to provide something that is unique." What drives inventors of a new product or service is the desire to bring this new thing before the public. They want to prove to themselves and to others that it is as valuable as at one point they may have been alone in thinking that it would be.

Never underestimate the creative pleasure that drives many who find their calling in business. Walking an interested stranger through their operations, they take as much pride in what they have built as any *diva* in a standing-ovation performance at La Scala. They remember what it was like when all this was nothing but a dream (concerning which, many sober people told them they would lose their shirt). Like the Creator in Genesis, they look over what they have made and find it good—but usually with a restless eye, trying to make it better.

↓ My friend Joe Jacobs, founder of Jacobs Engineering in Los Angeles (and author of the instructive book, *The Compassionate Conservative*), is bubbly and joyous about the fun he had building up his business. He has a sign on his desk, "BABE RUTH STRUCK OUT 1330 TIMES." Asked, he is glad to tell you about the many times that Joe Jacobs struck out too. At one point, when he tried to retire too early, things started to go wrong—some bad decisions were made—under the new chief executive officer, and personnel relations also deteriorated badly. Joe had really intended to retire and so stayed away from the company. By the time he was persuaded to return, after about four years, bankruptcy was near at hand. He had two choices: accept bankruptcy or cut personnel severely and swim as strongly as he could for solid land far ahead. Those he had to cut were guys he had hired and enjoyed being with, having known their wives and kids and all their family circumstances for years. The cutting was, he says, "gut-wrenching," the hardest thing he had ever had to do. Sink or swim, he kept telling himself. His only comfort—it wasn't much at the time—was that if he succeeded, he would save a good many other jobs; if he did nothing, the firm, and everybody with it, would go down.

In retrospect, Joe came to think he hadn't made all the right choices either. There were some people he let go who probably would have done a better job than one or two of those he kept. But the firm came out of it all right: much smaller and with bare cupboards for a while, but later stronger than ever. It's the pain, Joe suggests, that makes the later happiness of having built the firm so poignantly satisfying. You can't forget, later, all the costs, close brushes with disaster, bad days and nights. The hard and stormy things are as much a part of a calling as the cloudless ones. Emerging on the other side, you understand accomplishment in ways that in youth you did not expect. The 1330 strikeouts make the homers sweeter.

One reason people like a business calling, then, is the challenges it offers. They like the feeling, toward the end of life, that they were severely tested and accomplished something—something that they can see, that they know has made a contribution. They know this, because people use what they have provided, sometimes praise it, value it, pay good money for it—and are glad to do so. Joe can see the buildings, refineries, and countless other projects his firm has put up. He takes pride in their quality. But I think that most of all, he has enjoyed going through the hardships with his team and his association with them. Joe is both a people person and an excellence person—an engineer with lots of compassion. (He defines compassion by whether it helps the beneficiary to better his or her condition, or only makes the giver feel good; he is pretty passionate about the harm the latter does.)

✢ The unsung heroes of business, of course, are those in middle management who, when things get tough, as at Jacobs Engineering some years ago and in the current wave of restructuring, are the ones let go. Talk about the firm going down; what about their families? James H. Billington, Jr., an alert and inquisitive Episcopal seminarian who worked for five years in a large corporation—his aim was to form a ministry for people in business—has written eloquently:

> The middle manager faces a double bind. First, he is subject to the same religious/cultural conditioning as everyone else in a business, subtly teaching him that he is just in it for the money, that making money is bad, etc. But he is also subject to the disrespect of the business elite, who have been taught in the business schools that middle management is the reason that American companies cannot compete. But in fact most Americans who work in business are still middle managers. And middle management still makes up most of the jobs in business.

Most people in business are neither tightening bolts on engines nor sitting in the president's office. "Most people," Billington reminds us, "are still writing invoices or computer codes, running a department or sales force—working to implement plans that they did not create." They are still most of the people in the business world. "And NOWHERE," Billington concludes, "in the business literature that I have found is there any recognition of the legitimate, substantive and honorable contributions of the middle manager."

Well, I have found many and eloquent tributes to such people and their indispensability—on their retirement. Heads of firms certainly know who keeps their company surging ahead, or at least on even keel, and how helpless they are if their middle managers are incompetent or inattentive. Most pride themselves on recruiting, motivating, and amply rewarding top-flight managers, including a bunch of them capable of replacing the top honcho. Managerial talent is rare, and the extra margin of inventiveness and courage that make a great leader is even rarer.

Moreover, being a middle manager is not primarily a way station on the way to the top. Probably everyone wants at first to test themselves against that possibility; but, realistically, most middle managers expect some advancement over a lifetime, higher salaries and bonuses, and most of all the ever higher respect of their peers, while expecting to remain middle managers (vice-president tops) until retirement. Middle management, many know early, is their calling. They want to be super good at it. They want to make a contribution. Most of all, they need to know in their own minds that they have done so.

Second, their daily bread is recognition from their peers and those who work with them that they are very good at what they do. But they also want, as humans properly do, recognition from higher ups.

As the world goes, except for the few at the top (deservedly or undeservedly), most people do not get the recognition they have earned. "That's what's wrong with the world," an otherworldly and happy nun, Sister Gervase, told me in seventh grade. "People don't compliment other people enough. They would change the world if they did."

More than anyone else in business, middle managers are in the position to compliment those who work under them every day. The spirit they give the firm—if they are sustained by their superiors—*is* the firm in action. They are the chief community builders. They give (or fail to give) the firm its human character.

They are also the main trustees of the integrity and moral

practices of the firm. They are its moral and intellectual spine. Business is a noble field of work, and they are its chief day-to-day guardians. By their leadership, they make their bosses look good—or bad—and, in a slightly different way, they also make those who work under them look good—or bad. (Their leadership is nearly always more hands-on than that of those above them.) For all the solid, concrete things that business does for communities and for the entire nation, they are the down-to-earth leaders most responsible. For their success, they depend a lot on good leadership from the top, but it may also be argued that good leadership at the top depends even more disproportionately on them.

↓ The advertising executive Emilie Griffin presents another aspect of the business calling in her good book, *The Reflective Executive*. It is clear, she writes, "that the best entrepreneurial visions are founded in love." She uses the example of Phyllis Jordan, founder of PJ's Coffee and Tea Company, a regional enterprise that franchises coffee shops. PJ's is built around two different insights, each of them expressing in plain English an aspect of what religious people would call love—not the sentiment, but the effort to build community.

Phyllis Jordan explains why she started PJ's in this fashion:

↓ What I was really attracted to was being in the retail business. . . .

↓ I had a friend who was in the coffee business, that gave me the information I needed, the know-how. . . .

↓ But I think that sense of her in [her coffee shop], offering a product which was a shared experience with a friend, that was what attracted me to coffee. I wanted to see people talking to the people they've come with, or maybe the people they haven't come with. I don't think we can document this, but I know there are major social changes going on, including a return to basics, maybe concern about the environment, a number of things that are converging to make neighborhood experiences and simple values very important. I think specialty coffee in the U.S. is part of that.

This camaraderie in the coffee shop—a neighborhood place for a little sharing—is the central insight that animates Phyllis Jordan and PJ's, as other central insights animate scores of thousands of other entrepreneurs.

But Jordan has another central theme in mind, too—a worldwide one. She served for a year as president of the Specialty Coffee Association of America and saw another level of community at work:

> The [specialty coffee] association brings together people from growing countries and exporters and farmers with roasters and retailers in a trade association in which the focus is the product, and not on which part of the business you're in, and in that way it's a very cooperative effort, one that produces win-win solutions for growers and manufacturers and everybody. We think the organization can only work if everybody along the chain wins.

Here Emilie Griffin herself comments that "words such as these from a regional entrepreneur may have about them a sense of the commonplace, the ordinary." To her eye, though, this creative urge of enterprise can become a saintly one—in the perfectly natural sense of saintliness: "When the reflective executive strives to live out his or her inner vision through a sharing of values, not only with co-workers and customers, not only with colleagues and others in industry, but with the world in the largest possible definition or conception of which he or she is capable."

Jordan may not want her words to fly so high, and yet what she does matters more than what she says. She enjoys building community, on more than one level. That sort of calling seems to please something deep within her. She sees her daily work— "what I liked was the tremendous variety of tasks"—in a far larger framework. Entrepreneurs often see a little more in humble things than other people do. Their characteristic habit is sharp discernment.

⅄ In this vein, Paul F. Oreffice, retired chairman of the Dow Chemical Company, says that his greatest satisfaction in business was working with and knowing the "guys" in middle management—always on his lookout for talent. He remembers spotting a thirty-one-year old researcher who became a "gigantic" strength for the company. His greatest pride lies in having spotted eight special talents among younger fellows in the company in 1975 and pushing them along. From this list of eight, he said with satisfaction almost twenty years later, seven were now in the top leadership of the firm.

"Never chew out a colleague in public," he says. "The idea is to create a team. And to form in them the habit of not bringing you their problems. The only question I had for each of them was, 'What's your *solution?*' They have to be the ones to make the decisions. They have to learn to talk things through in a team—one brain is never as good as four or five brains."

He also says: "If a guy doesn't look at business as a vocation, he's not gonna make it. And the vocation changes as you grow. For me, it was one thing at 30, another at 50 and at 60. The one consistent thing—I loved challenges."

Paul was born in Italy, and as a child emigrated with his parents to Ecuador. His first business success was turning a small chemical company in Brazil into the nation's second largest in the field. He was twenty-eight when he started on that challenge.

He loved his years at Dow, turning down offers to work elsewhere, always being given new challenges. He liked working for a company—"founded by a farm boy from Nebraska"—that had a tradition of never, under any circumstances, paying bribes or going under the table with officials. "The rule was there: That made it easy for those who came later. No ifs, ands, or buts."

It is obvious that Mr. Oreffice—twice an immigrant, to Latin America and to the United States—loved his time in business.

↓ John W. Rowe of New England Electric System remembers thinking that money is not what really motivated him when, one day, between two jobs, he was standing at a newsstand in an airport. He saw a copy of *Playboy* and distinctly recalls telling himself that he could understand people buying it and enjoying it, "but I don't really wish to make my living selling it." It's important to value the business you're in and to take satisfaction from providing its services or goods to others. At the end of the day, you want to respect what you do. In a certain sense, our work *is* us. We get into it, and it gets into us.

There is nothing wrong with wanting to make a good living, or even in seeking out a life of business that produces good rewards. But not all ways of gaining money are equal. Better than inheriting money is to earn it through inventiveness and hard work—or at least to make something better of it, using it well. Business is about creating goods and services, jobs and benefits, and new wealth that didn't exist before. In choosing a line of work, you want to find the one that suits the kind of person you are—the individual you are. Mr. Rowe is very much oriented toward free market ideas, although his business (natural gas) is a halfway house between entrepreneurship and nonprofit government activity. In this mix, the government and politics side can be especially irritating, because it seems to be moved more often by transient emotion than by long-term reason. Perhaps this explains the slight vehemence Mr. Rowe showed when a pastor in Maine came by to see him when he was at an earlier job with a utility company.

After discussing the main item on his agenda, the pastor asked Mr. Rowe, more or less by way of chitchat, how he liked his job. Mr. Rowe replied: "Oh, I like it. It gives me a chance to work with people I respect, who know a lot that I don't know. I get to protect capital from some of the depredations of government. Most of all, I like to think I'm helping to keep an important part of our economic infrastructure in place, in support of other people's opportunities."

Mr. Rowe still remembers the stunned look on the minister's face: "You mean you have a calling?"

FOUR CHARACTERISTICS OF A CALLING

What have we learned about callings from these examples? At least four points should now be clear, about callings in general and those in business in particular.

First, each calling is unique to each individual. Not everyone wants to be a psychiatrist, as Dr. Peck discovered. Nor, for that matter, does everyone want to work in business. Each of us is as unique in our calling as we are in being made in the image of God. (It would take an infinite number of human beings, St. Thomas Aquinas once wrote, to mirror back the infinite facets of the Godhead. Each person reflects only a small—but beautiful—part of the whole.)

Second, a calling requires certain preconditions. It requires more than desires; it requires talent. Not everyone can be, simply by desiring it, an opera singer, or professional athlete, or leader of a large enterprise. For a calling to be right, it must fit our abilities. Another precondition is love—not just love of the final product but, as the essayist Logan Pearsall Smith once put it, "The test of a vocation is love of drudgery it involves." Long hours, frustrations, small steps forward, struggles: unless these too are welcomed with a certain joy, the claim to being called has a hollow ring.

Third, a true calling reveals its presence by the enjoyment and sense of renewed energies its practice yields us. This does not mean that sometimes we do not groan inwardly at the weight of the burdens imposed on us or that we never feel reluctance about reentering bloody combat. Facing hard tasks necessarily exacts dread. Indeed, there are times when we wish we did not have to face every burden our calling imposes on us. Still, finding ourselves where we are and with the responsibilities we bear, we know it is our duty—part of what we were meant to do—to soldier on.

Enjoying what we do is not always a feeling of enjoyment; it is sometimes the gritty resolution a man or woman shows in doing what must be done—perhaps with inner dread and yet without whimpering self-pity. These are things a grown man or woman must do. There is an odd satisfaction in bearing certain pains. The young men who died defending the pass at Thermopylae, Aristotle intimates, died happy. But he was not describing their feelings, only their knowledge that they did what brave young Spartans ought to do to protect their city, no matter the taste of ashes in their mouths.

A fourth truth about callings is also apparent: they are not usually easy to discover. Frequently, many false paths are taken before the satisfying path is at last uncovered. Experiments, painful setbacks, false hopes, discernment, prayer, and much patience are often required before the light goes on.

Businesspeople who have found their calling will recognize all of these things, if only tacitly. Against sometimes dreary opposition, they know their calling to be morally legitimate, even noble. Listen again to the testimony heard in this chapter. The point of business is "to accomplish something collectively," "to make a contribution to society," "to do something which is of value," "to provide something that is unique," "to test a person's talents and character," "to build community." This is unambiguously moral language that reflects moral reality.

The rest of this book puts flesh on the bones of the callings briefly glimpsed here. At least four themes concerning the moral nature of business have thus far risen to the surface: (1) Business is able to build praiseworthy forms of community. (2) A life in business is creative; it can transform the conditions of human life dramatically and for the better (or the worse). (3) Business is a source of endless personal challenge, testing intellectual and moral mettle in the crucible of practicality. (4) Those practicing it often see business as a way of giving back to society, both through the goods and services it produces and in philanthropy, through the new wealth it generates.

All of these themes will surface in the chapters to come. But before we start exploring them from the inside out, we need to answer two more questions about the nature of a calling. Can a calling remain implicit and unspoken? Is there such a thing as a secular, nonreligious calling?

CAN A CALLING REMAIN TACIT?

I know from talking to and corresponding with businesspeople that many have never been asked whether they regard what they do as a calling. They don't think about themselves that way. That has not been the language of the business schools, the economics textbooks, or the secularized public speech of our time. (In previous generations, public speech in America was frequently biblical and Shakespearean.) But most of them, they say, do start mulling the idea of calling once it is raised. Some confess that they could think of what they do as a calling, even if they have not. That would not be much of a reach from what they have already been doing. It's just one of those things that, so far, too few people say.

But they could, and it would be better if they did. It would give them a greater sense of being part of a noble profession. It would raise their own esteem for what they do—and no doubt stimulate their imaginations about how they might gain greater and deeper satisfactions from doing it. It would help tie them more profoundly to traditions going far back into the past, in seeing their own high place in the scheme of things. The human project is a universal project. We are involved in bringing the Creator's work to its intended fulfillment by being co-creators in a very grand project, indeed. In this, we are tied to the whole human race.

In particular, business has a special role to play in bringing hope—and not only hope, but actual economic progress—to the billion or so truly indigent people on this planet. Business is, bar none, the best real hope of the poor. And that is one of the noblest callings inherent in business activities: to raise up the poor.

CAN A CALLING BE ENTIRELY SECULAR?

Yes. That answer rests on the evidence of fact. Among America's well-educated elites especially, many people do think in nonreligious terms. (Frequently they do not recognize that many of today's secular terms are derived from religious precedents. However, we would not speak of secularization unless our basic terms had first been religious.) As far as they can see, there is no one or nothing calling them. Indeed, they know from experience the difference between going down one road in search of their own proper career for a while and recognizing it as a mistake, then turning in a new direction. They know what it is like to "find themselves"— to find the activities they are good at and thoroughly enjoy and feel at home doing. They are quite capable of using what seems to them to be a wholly secular language. In addition, religious language may make some of them uncomfortable; it feels false.

For most citizens of the world, however, the background language of their self-awareness springs from the originality and distinctive dramaturgy of the biblical vision of cosmic history. For some three thousand years, both unbelievers and those affected by the biblical vision (the Koran accepts the Jewish and Christian testaments as its starting place) have engaged in rival picturings and theory building in trying to interpret human life. But we all must deal with the same facts of human experience, so there is much overlap in our interpretations. It is fair to say that how the West thinks about life has been mainly shaped (for a majority of the peoples of the world) by Judaism, Christianity, and Islam.

Even the philosophical riches of pagan Greece and Rome, buried under the ferocity of the barbarian invasions from the fourth century on, were recovered for the West under the aegis of Jewish, Christian, and Muslim rulers, scholars, and artists. In all three of these great shaping forces of the human imagination, moreover, one fundamental point is the same: the Creator of all things knows the name of each of us—knows thoroughly, better than we do ourselves, what is in us, for he put it there and intends for us to do something with it—something that meshes with his intentions for many other people. This proposition, suitably rephrased, is capable of standing as a distinctively secular worldview.

Nothing is by chance, these religions teach, in the sense of being beyond his knowing of it, although certainly in life there are many crossing lines of contingency that set off those sparks of surprise, spontaneity, and unplannedness that we call chance. In this respect, religious believers and secular unbelievers might see the same realities but interpret their meaning differently.

Further, for the three major religions mentioned, God does not pull puppets' strings. He made free creatures to govern themselves freely. Still, in freely improvising our parts in the drama of our lives, we must plainly draw on the unique resources with which he endowed each of us. All this, too, has been rethought and reexpressed in secular analogues.

Religious persons imagine that the Creator is disappointed if we fail to live up to what we are capable of—at least as disappointed as we ourselves are likely to be. It is hard to hide such disappointment from ourselves if it is present, even if subconsciously. But secular persons, examining themselves as if from the viewpoint of an impartial spectator, may feel the same disappointment.

In our civilization, then, more secularized than it used to be, atheists and agnostics and those who are just not particularly religious (or tone-deaf regarding religion) are likely to have just as strong a sense of calling as religious persons, although they would not use the word *God*. After all, the God they don't believe in tends to be the God of Judaism, Christianity, and Islam, and the "self" they do know about is of the same cultural inheritance as that of believers. Though they are likely to speak of knowing themselves, finding their own identity, seeking their own fulfillment, even "doing their own thing," what they are doing is very like responding to a calling.

Put more strongly, the secular language of self-knowledge, identity, self-fulfillment, and the pursuit of (personal) happiness has been so interblended with the traditional Jewish-Christian-Muslim sense of calling for thousands of years that it is not easy to pull them apart. Within limits, all of us are talking about pretty much the same thing. We are probably flexible enough to try on each other's language and to translate from one to the other as needed.

METEORITES ACROSS THE SKY

People in business are not merely "rational economic agents." Each is also a human being in search of his calling. All are trying to live fulfilled lives, eager to mix their own identity with their work and their work with their identity. They want more satisfactions from work than money.

Further, people in business are not merely objects of analysis; they are subjects. They have other purposes in their economic activities than merely economic ones; they have other dimensions of their being to satisfy. More than that, they are ends in themselves. The soul of each of us is, in the words of the poet, "immortal diamond."

And the most important thing people wish to satisfy cannot be generalized because it is as unique to every person as an individual's DNA.

There is no more beautiful thing in the universe than the human person. What shows each of us to be distinctive is the trajectory of the calling we pursue, like meteorites across the night sky of history.

Chapter Two

✧

LITTLE-KNOWN FACTS
ABOUT BUSINESS

Despite certain Talmudic sayings to the contrary, no anticommercial tradition existed in Judaism. . . . Man's earning of a livelihood and his creation of economic and material assets are seen as the reflections of Divine pleasure. Leafing through the pages of the Bible, one is immediately struck by the fact that the observance of God's commandments leads to an abundance of material goods. . . . A God fearing man is characterized as one whose flocks and orchards bear their fruit in season and produce a bounty of goods. . . . the high priest offered a special prayer in the Temple, the major component of which is a request for a year of bounty, a year in which Jews will not have to be dependent on others for their livelihood.

—Meir Tamari

Islam protects and endorses the personal right to own what one may freely gain, through legitimate means, such as gifts and the fruits of the labor of one's hand or intellect. It is a sacred right. Yet, human ownership is tempered by the understanding that everything, in the last analysis, belongs to God, including our souls and bodies, as well as the means of our living, which God has created for our benefit. What appears to be ownership is in fact a matter of trusteeship . . .

—Muhammed Abdul-Rauf

AN OVERVIEW

In the United States, the latest figures, for 1994, show that 123 million Americans are gainfully employed. Some 18 million of them work for government (federal, state, or local). A rough estimate of those who work for various sorts of nonprofit organizations—schools and universities, museums, research institutes, clinics and hospitals, and the like—is 5 million. In other words, something like 100 million people work for businesses of various kinds. About 11.5 million are employed by the Fortune 500 companies. The others mostly work for small businesses. There are now more than 17 million sole proprietorships and small partnerships, up from 5.8 million in 1970; but only 2 to 3 million of these pay additional wages. Including farmers, some 10.6 million Americans are self-employed.

In 1970, there were only 60 million employed persons in the United States. In just twenty-five years, the United States has more than doubled the number of jobs. Most of these jobs have been created by small businesses, the economy's most dynamic sector. Most new employment is in this sector, which is also the major seedbed for new inventions, technologies, and services. During the 1980s, small businesses created over 20 million jobs, while Fortune 500 companies cut 3.5 million jobs. (In 1975, the Fortune 500 employed 16 million persons, compared to 11.5 million in 1993.)

Additionally, entirely new industries have come into existence since 1970: semiconductors, computers, robotics, fax machines, cellular phones, compact discs, cable television companies, fiber optics, genetic pharmaceuticals, and countless numbers and types of service industries. Many of these industries originated in very small firms.

For Jews, Christians, Muslims, and others, the amazing growth of business activities is the major economic fact of the twentieth century. In 1900, almost 11 million of the 29 million employed Americans worked on farms, and several million others in related occupations. More than half the labor force lived in farming communities. In 1993, not quite a century later, fewer than 2 million Americans were employed in agriculture. (More than half of those were employed in agribusiness, not family farming.) During more than two thousand years, the life of farming was the basic economic reality for both the poor and the aristocracy. In that perspective, the great economic transformation from agriculture to business has been abrupt. Moral and religious thinkers have not yet adjusted their imaginations to this upheaval.

THE MOST RELIGIOUS ELITES

Of all the elites of American society—social scientists, artists, humanists, the military, athletes, politicians, movie stars, journalists, lawyers, and others—the military, athletes, and people of business appear to rank among the most religious. Not all persons in business are religious, but a high proportion are. A great number of them, though they get little affirmation for their vocations from the clergy or the general culture, are confident that the work they do is moral. Many of them want to do it in a way as faithful to their religious faith and religious longings as they can. Many are delighted to find people who take their religious inclinations seriously.

In a poll of twelve American elites in 1990, sociologists Stanley Rothman and Robert Lerner of Smith College discovered that next to military officers (and leaving aside church professionals), more people in business attended church every week than any other elite: twice as many as congressional aides, four times more than people in the news media, nine times more than television and movie elites. Thirty-five percent of people in business attended church weekly and another 15 percent once a month; only 13 percent replied "never." Compare that with public interest elites, of whom only 10 percent attended church every week while 37 percent never did.

Aside from the clergy, the military are the best at getting to church: 46 percent weekly, and only 13 percent never. The people in the movie industry are the worst: only 4 percent every week and 63 percent never. (See the table.)

I have not been able to get exact numbers on athletes, but games seen on television display extraordinary signs of religiousness among athletes: kneeling in thanksgiving, crossing themselves, and speaking of God in interviews, for example. The organization of prayer meetings and Bible study groups on individual teams, and even in national associations, suggests as well a high degree of formal commitment.

CHURCH ATTENDANCE BY ELITE GROUP

	Every Week	Once a Month	A Few Times a Year	Never	(N in Sample)
Movies	4%	1%	32%	63%	91
TV	4	3	49	44	104
News media	9	6	37	48	236
Public interest elites	10	7	46	37	156
Corporate lawyers	15	16	46	24	148
Congressional aides	17	17	45	21	134
Federal judges	17	20	51	12	113
Bureaucrats	25	12	33	30	196
Labor union members	31	19	40	11	95
Business	35	15	37	13	239
Military officers	46	21	25	13	239
Religious professionals	92	6	2	0	178

Percentage greater than 100 due to rounding.
Source: Center for the Study of Social and Political Change

We can speculate that professions that put their members at considerable risk—the military, athletes, people in business—impress on them their dependence on many factors beyond their own control. Such persons know what it is like to have Lady Fortune blowing into their sails one day, and on another to see those sails fall slack. They know what it is like to *depend*. The biblical language of trusting in Providence seems to such persons realistic.

Further, some spiritual exercises produce a kind of inner cleansing, centering, and equanimity; perceptibly, these help people to perform at the top of their form. To such persons, religion makes sense. So do traditional virtues. Joe Paterno of Penn State—a former teacher of the classics—has written eloquently of the relevance of the Greek and Latin virtues to the world of football athletes.

By contrast, the professions of the "adversary culture" (those who think themselves superior, such as the media) seem to diminish religious energies and deplete religious curiosity. Some secularized professionals exude a polite but unmistakable hostility to religion. This keeps the media, in particular, well out of touch with American popular culture. Conversely, people in business—especially in small business, in suburbs and small towns—remain very close to other ordinary Americans. The latter are among the most religious people in the world, both in belief and in weekly (even daily) practices. About 42 percent of all American adults attend church weekly.

More people in the United States attend religious services on any given weekend than watch football—in all the stadiums, on high school football fields, college campuses, and all the television sets of the nation put together. Four of the ten greatest television audiences ever were registered by professional football Superbowls, yet fewer people were in those television audiences on those Superbowl Sundays than attended church that morning.

TODAY MOST RELIGIOUS PEOPLE
WORK IN BUSINESS

A second premise on which I build is that a large proportion of the laypersons in this world today, perhaps even a substantial majority, work out their destiny—economic, social, and religious— in the daily activities of business. I do not mean only the entrepreneurs—the small farmers, the shopowners, the multiplying numbers of consultants working at their word processors and computers in independent businesses, the barbers and hairdressers, the managers of large firms, the corporate executives—but all those others who work with them and whose daily bread depends on the success of business activities. "Doing business" is what most citizens in free nations do most of the time. Business is the meat and potatoes of most "living in the world" today and will be even more so in the daily life of the twenty-first century, as more and more nations turn to free market activities as the main economic occupation of civil societies.

All the lands of the former Soviet Union, nearly all the nations of Latin America, and large swathes of Asia and Africa are entering the global marketplace. Hopefully, that marketplace will steadily become lawlike and peaceful. *Commercium et Pax*, commerce and peace, was the proud motto of Amsterdam, one of the first great market societies of the modern world, whose busy port was crowded with the dipping and swaying masts of sailing vessels coming from nearly every harbor of the globe. Commerce is what people do when they are at peace.

Commerce, as several of the Eastern fathers of the Catholic church wrote, notably St. John Chrysostom, is the material bond among peoples that exhibits, as if symbolically, the unity of the whole human race—or, as he dared to put it in mystical language, shows forth in a material sign the "mystical Body of Christ." The human race is one. The international commerce that shows forth the interdependence of all parts of the human body knits the peoples of the world together by the silken threads of a seamless garment.

Commerce is dignified by this mysterious and often inadvertent activity—this knitting together of the nations, to which we all too seldom explicitly lift our gaze. In our local activities, which are often so difficult and challenging that we scarcely have time to contemplate their larger meaning, we are engaged, often unknowingly, in weaving a small but crucial part of the universal tapestry. We are part of something much larger than ourselves. We are bringing together the entire human race, activating our local part of the universal work of the noble, wounded race to which it is our glory to belong.

We are trying to wrest from the ashes of war and division the hard-burnished alloys of peace: an elemental prosperity for all, the rule of law, and daily practices of freely given consent.

War is a destroyer; commerce is a builder. Division, separation, and isolation unravel the substance of human unity; lawlike and mutually respectful commerce knits human societies together into one.

In addition, commerce works in a humble but privileged way. It ties together persons who have never met one another. The very impersonality that Marx excoriated as the "cash nexus" is the humble glory of commerce. Commerce does not require that we have physical or emotional contact with all with whom we do business.

Consider the pipe in my cabinet that I wish I were smoking (my doctor has required that I no longer use it). I know not where the exotic wood of its bowl comes from, or who with such art designed it or turned it out; or whence the rubber of its stem was drawn or by whom processed; or where the metal ring that separates the two was produced; or from which pits of ore the substances from which it was alloyed derive; or who invented the filter designed to allow hot smoke to exit halfway to the mouthpiece; or who arranged for the multiple transactions that brought all these elements together for the manufacturer who sold it (direct from the factory) to me. Without having met them, I have often felt gratitude to them.

What languages all the workers in this farflung set of enterprises speak I know not, or how they address their God, or their thoughts or feelings.

From all over the world, we have been brought together—those who make and those who enjoy the fruit of their labors and inventions. By many invisible paths, with no one knowing or intending all the human relations by which it passed into my hands, and perhaps without any one person in the world having all the knowledge, arts, and skills required in all the steps of its journey to my cabinet, we have nonetheless been brought together in the pleasures my pipe has afforded me. To all these unknown persons I give thanks. In my hands I have held tangible evidence of the world community to which we belong.

This same evidence teaches me that I have obligations to them, though I do not know who they are.

In this way, commerce is the most solid, material sign of unmistakable human solidarity. And yet it takes away from none of us our cultural differences, not to mention our individuality. I think of my pipe as a "peace pipe," not only for the pacifying effect its use once brought me, but also for the sense of universal community it evokes, together with the latter's obligations.

Perhaps because I am Catholic, my mind works naturally in such sacramental ways. Everything around us is a sign of the beyond. We have merely to allow our natural wonderment free reign. "Everything we look upon is blest" (Yeats). "Everything is grace" (Bernanos). But one does not have to be Catholic to grasp this method. I think it must be natural to humans.

MORALITY AND US

Many people in America and other advanced countries today think of morality apart from religion. Like the ancient Greeks and Romans, they have learned from experience about self-destructive and, by contrast, long-term, life-enhancing activities; about vice and virtue and character and the like. They speak of such matters without using (or feeling the need of) religious language. Some of them are religious in other ways, although hardly so in moral thinking. Others are tone-deaf regarding religion; it does little for them, they will tell you.

For most of us in America, morality is first taught to us not as morality but rather as religion. The language that many of us were first taught is relational. It has to do with our relation to a Person, to the Almighty, to God. Our moral life is surrounded with a sense of the sacred. Morality is not just an abstract list of do's and don'ts. It is a sense that there is One who calls us to himself and that doing wrong is far worse than merely stepping across a line derived from an abstract principle. It is to give injury to One who made us and loves us.

Moreover, to do wrong is to do injury to ourselves, to violate a call we have received in our very being. Morality is not extrinsic to us. It is designed into the very aspirations (and temptations) of our being. It plunges us into an inner war with rival, and sometimes inharmonious, tendencies in our own soul.

I do not think this is a singularly Catholic way of looking at things. Socrates and Plato speak of the luminous Good drawing our souls onward by its breathtaking beauty, to become all that we can be. The Jewish testament speaks of the law as a "lamp unto my feet," "a way," an illuminated "path," a matter of covenant and, therefore, of fidelity to a solemn mutual promise made to each other by the Creator and his children.

Thus, when I wrote about morality as a matter of unique personality, I was far from speaking about it as outside living moral traditions and moral communities. It is true that we must each appropriate, that is, make our own, the tradition into which we have been born. Otherwise, the tradition does not truly root itself in us but remains extrinsic to us.

Besides, if enough members of a community fail to appropriate their tradition in fresh and vital ways, that tradition ceases by so much to live, except as in a remnant. Traditions can become dead letters. Many have.

Again, though morality is personal and concrete, it does not escape from the power of general laws and absolute "thou shalt nots." There are some things that humans simply must not do, without forfeiting their own claim to human dignity. Some things are always and everywhere absolutely unworthy of them.

Not long ago, after Pope John Paul II had made a claim of just that sort (in his encyclical on truth and liberty, *Veritatis Splendor*), a friend of mine was defending the good sense of that claim on a liberal talk show. A modern, "progressive" Catholic on the air with him, a pro-choice ex-nun, as she made clear, called such a view medieval and defied him to name a single absolute moral prescription. Without having had time to think of a better one, he found himself saying: "Thou shalt not rape." That inspired reply resulted in an awkward silence at the other microphone.

Most of those today who boast that they are relativists have their own code of absolutes. Being a total relativist is far harder than most imagine; it is a demanding vocation to try to live.

What we mean by "goodwill" is the ardent desire of those who are perplexed for light in which to discover just exactly what they ought to do. Often enough, far too often, we know that we would like to do the right thing, yet for the life of us, what that is seems dismayingly obscure. Sometimes in those obscurities, we come to recognize that in the need to make a sudden choice, we chose the wrong thing. We didn't mean to, but we blew it. Such experiences make us anxious the next time the mists of obscurity cloud our moral vision. Seeing clearly is often half the problem. Having the will to *do* it is, at other times, the other half.

THE ONLY MORAL MAJORITY: SINNERS

Lest that last comment be misleading, I hasten to add that this book is not written for saints but for fellow strugglers. Many of us meet a number of holy persons in our lives (sometimes in our own families), persons who endure great sufferings with quiet grace and cheerfulness, and persons of extraordinary gifts of the spirit. We do not count ourselves among them. We belong to the only moral majority there is: sinners.

Yet we do want to live our lives for God, the best we can—perhaps as a way of thanking him, perhaps as a way of making the best use we can of the talents he has given us, perhaps because we simply feel within us a mysterious call to which, in a certain darkness of the soul, we try to answer.

At this point, a word is needed on our diversity of faiths—or, better, "standpoints," including those of nonbelievers. Although we in America are lucky to live under a constitutional structure that allows freedom of conscience to all, and thereby confers on us the privilege of living and working peaceably with persons whose faith is different from our own, we often feel the impulse to lift the bushel a little so that the light from our own faith may shine out from it. We should do so. And so should others. It would be a mistake on all our parts if we let pluralism mean that we each hid from every other, and from the public square, what is most important to us.

Our faiths—all the classic faiths—are not a merely private matter. They are intended to enrich the human spirit in its public as well as its private reaches. Without attempting to coerce one another, or even to trespass on one another's sensitivities, we should when the occasion presents itself reveal at least a little of our deepest moral and religious longings, so as to share these with those closest to us. We can help one another in this way, knitting bonds of mutual depth and common understanding. Mere back slapping is not enough.

Democracy is undoubtedly the best system the world has ever known for diminishing abuses of individuals and minorities, but every system, including democracy, is morally problematic. Democracies, in particular, must make special efforts to protect high public ideals, for it is an inexorable tendency of democracies to pull public morals downward, as popular television does today.

In older societies, the aristocracy committed many gross abuses. Still, despite the sins of its members, the aristocracy qua aristocracy usually performed the institutional function of setting high public ideals, undeterred by public opinion. Without such institutional bracing, the common taste is typically vulnerable to a downward drift. A rush to the bottom is easily set in motion, for the vulgar instinctively make fun of, and easily intimidate, those above them, who in a democracy fear being labeled as "undemocratic" or "elitist."

Like the aristocratic society, like all other regimes, democratic society has inherent weaknesses, and maintaining high moral ideals in its central institutions is one of them. Other regimes may more often suffer from corruption—"power corrupts"—but democracy must strain vigorously against the slippery slope of popular passion and taste.

For that reason, those of us who live in democratic societies have special need to strengthen one another, especially in matters of the spirit, religion, morals, and, on a lesser but still important level, even manners and taste. To keep our own standards high, we need one another.

This book may be taken as an effort to give such encouragement to others—and in return to gain it.

✧

If Tocqueville was correct, that democracies are ever in danger of slipping downward from high ideals in moral and cultural life, it is imperative that the sound ideals animating the business calling—ideals of community, creativity, practical realism, self-discovery, and many others—be more fully articulated. As we have seen, these ideals may be quite invigorating and challenging. Further, given that so many democratic citizens work in business, and given their sense that what they do is morally legitimate, to ignore or cover over the moral dimension of business is to suck wind out of the democratic sail, and to watch the experiment in self-government go slack.

The *mystique* of democracy wins hearts easily, yet as the French poet Charles Péguy has written, *mystique* over time degenerates into *politique*—the outer mechanics of government bureaucracies, without soul. In the project of self-government, business is without doubt the single largest institution of civil society. The moral health of society, therefore, depends to a great extent on the moral character of business leaders.

To observe the high moral stakes involved—not to mention the inescapable moral ambiguities—we turn to one of the most extraordinary businessmen of American (and world) history, Andrew Carnegie.

Chapter Three

✧

A MORALLY SERIOUS CALLING

Tell Mr. Carnegie I'll see him in hell, where we both are
going.
> —*Henry Clay Frick,*
> *last message to Andrew Carnegie, 1901*

Anybody who goes to business school gets used to being put
down by friends in the liberal arts or social sciences: "So what
are you in it for? To make a buck?" The implication is that any
other field of study is morally worthy, but to study business—
worse, to engage in it—is crass. It is not so much that others
think that business should not be engaged in or even that they
themselves are not interested in making a buck. They are. But
they have been taught—we all have, since at least the times of
the ancient Greeks and Romans—that commerce is a faintly
smelly enterprise, lower in dignity than other callings.

Moreover, from the first glimmerings of the "social problem" in Europe—the problem of the poor, which German
thinkers labeled *Das Sozialproblem* at the beginning of the nineteenth century—the intellectuals of the world have marched
against free markets under the banner of equality. Thus, those
who make money, especially if they make lots of it, were
thought to be by definition part of the problem, rather than the
beginning of the solution. Intellectuals have rejoiced ever since
in defining the business class as their number one class enemy,
the epitome and cause of social evil.

This was a profound and serious intellectual error, and the
world has been suffering its ill effects ever since. Moreover,
since at least R. H. Tawney, the only motive many intellectuals
and clergy can conceive of for people in industry and commerce is greed—or, in Tawney's more aristocratic term, acquisitiveness. How often in a day do you read about "greed" or
hear about it on television? Yet making a living, even making a
very good living, even creating a lot of new wealth (also for
oneself), is not necessarily a sign of greed or even of upscale
acquisitiveness.

It is not wrong to want to be rich. It may be foolish—the
rich are not notably happier than the nonrich—but it is not
wrong. Getting anything you wish any time you wish is often
deadly to happiness—and also to achievement. Most of those
in business who become rich try to live as though they were
not, at least in two senses: they keep working hard, and they
seek out new challenges. Only a few of them become hedo-
nists, voluptuaries, gourmets, bon vivants, epicureans, or even
members of the "idle rich." Further, many of the successful see
the damage that being idle does to members of their families.
Being rich can be its own punishment.

It deprives you of excuses, for example. If a rich woman
really wanted to, she could do many things that other people
cannot even be tempted by, because they cannot afford to do

them, whereas she can. Such a woman is likely to feel guilty if she *isn't* happy, whereas poorer women find happiness where they can. Given her resources, she feels she should be able to make herself happy, but is uncertain what to *do*. A fierce dilemma always stares her in the face: "Since I can do anything I wish, what is worth spending my time on?"

Being rich is not a condition to be envied. Nonetheless, to want to be rich is no sin. It may be a self-condemnation, since the rich are so often empty and unhappy, but it is no sin. One can imagine wise people inventing ways to make being rich a good way to save one's soul, to live a worthwhile and good life, and even to have fun by taking on new challenges. But this path cannot be easy. Compared to the challenges faced by those without resources, the rich (unless they do something about it) are protected from risk. Being rich can take away crucial human challenges. Self-made people seem to be the happiest. They are often the most grateful, and most fulfilled.

A common sentiment expressed by artists and intellectuals, among others, is that it is unfair that some people are rich, while others aren't. This is an odd view of the world—a fantasy—since there has never been a society that is "fair" by that standard, and it is hard to imagine how there could be. Notwithstanding that, some intellectuals take the proposition "all men are created equal" as an argument against wealth. This is a European conception. It misses the American idea that by dint of imagination and sheer luck, individuals will begin with their native endowments and apply them unequally.

The American emphasis on equal *opportunity* assumes that not all will use these opportunities equally; and thus this principle further implies *inequality* in efforts and outcomes. If all outcomes were equal, extraordinary personal efforts would be in vain.

In short, inequality of outcomes is at the core of two pivotal American concepts: freedom and opportunity. Differential success is a crucial measure of freedom. "Created equal" means that nothing in one's class status at birth prevents one from seizing opportunity. It does not mean that everyone begins with the same family inheritance at birth or that what we have achieved during our lifetime must be limited to what we began with at birth.

In the American tradition, the term *equal* is properly defined by contrast with feudalism, specifically its way of ascribing differences of legal status at birth. The term is wrongly defined to signify "fairness as equality of incomes." That is a Continental, socialist, and false rendering of the American creed.

It is a further error to imagine that being wealthy produces greater happiness and human satisfaction. Despite their often-expressed personal idealism, many critics of the rich are regularly guilty of vulgar materialism in their contemplation of the wealthy. People who talk much about the "greed" of the rich, whether the latter's wealth is personally earned or merely inherited, are sometimes expressing the sour feelings of their own envy. But they misunderstand reality. As my father taught me, the rich should not be envied; we should feel sorry for them and pray for them.

Personal achievement—the fulfillment of a personal calling—means more than money in the measure of a human life. Some on the left recognize this; they speak a bit more kindly of those who earned their wealth by talent and application than of those who merely inherited it.

In addition, if the huge numbers of the poor in the world are ever to lift themselves out of poverty, they need those with ideas and capital to invest in creating the industries, jobs, and wealth that will give the poor a base to build on. Opportunities and jobs are more valuable to them than handouts from a government that treats them like serfs.

The ultimate complaint against the wealthy that rankles in

the bellies of some is that the *system* that produces inequalities
of wealth is wicked. This is the opposite of James Madison's
view; he thought that the passion for equality is the wicked project. Who is right? Let us consider the hatred that leftists, particularly leftists in Britain, had for Andrew Carnegie.

ANDREW CARNEGIE, WEALTH CREATOR

In a nasty reply to an article by Andrew Carnegie, then thought
to be one of world's greatest industrialists and the founder of
the modern corporation, the Reverend Hugh Price Hughes, a
noted Methodist minister in England, wrote in 1891: "When I
contemplate [Carnegie] as the representative of a particular
class of millionaires, I am forced to say, with all personal
respect, and without holding him in the least responsible for his
unfortunate circumstances, that he is an anti-Christian phe-
nomenon, a social monstrosity, and a grave political peril."
That's more or less putting it out where the horses can get it.

The reason the Reverend Hughes offered for his biting criticism is that Carnegie did not deal with the "fundamental question of society," which in Hughes's mind was the distribution of
wealth. A more temperate but highly similar analysis was
offered by William Jewett Tucker, a noted liberal theologian
from New England, professor of religion at Andover Seminary,
and later the distinguished president of Dartmouth. True
enough, Tucker wrote, Carnegie argued that the rich should
give away their money before they died—a noble and perhaps
useful deed—but he was still missing the "whole question of
economic justice now before society, and relegating it to the
field of charity, leaving the question of the original distribution
of wealth unsettled, or settled only to the satisfaction of the
few." He went on: "The ethical question of today centres, I am
sure, in the distribution rather than in the redistribution [i.e.,
voluntary giving away] of wealth."

The learned doctor was not quite exact, of course. Andrew Carnegie had no part in the "original distribution of wealth." He was born quite poor, in the small town of Dumferline in Scotland in 1835, and became much poorer when his father lost his cottage loom to the growing textile industry and brought the family, nearly penniless, to Pittsburgh, Pennsylvania. There, at age twelve, Andrew almost instantly had to go to work to help support the family. It is quite certain that Andrew Carnegie was born much poorer than the Reverend Doctor Tucker and, indeed, that Andrew was lucky if he caught even four years of formal schooling, compared to the formidable schooling of the future president of Dartmouth. Despite his limited education, Carnegie eventually became, reputedly, the "richest man in the world" when he sold all his interests to the newly formed U.S. Steel Corporation for $480 million in 1901 and promptly retired, at age sixty-six. He spent his last eighteen years, until his death in 1919, giving away his entire fortune, as he had promised to do at the age of thirty-three.

Yet Carnegie's staggering wealth as of 1901—it kept growing until his death—owed nothing to an "original distribution." Neither had he robbed banks or otherwise gained his fortune immorally or illegally. He invented wholly new ways of making iron, then later steel, and above all wholly new ways of organizing and administering a business.

Carnegie introduced scientific methods into smelting practices that had hitherto relied on a kind of intuition, alchemic "magic," and "touch." He was especially a genius at identifying genius in others, particularly in men born poor and largely unschooled, and with novel methods motivating them and winning the undying affection of most of them. As even his detractors noted, he practically singlehandedly (with his team) changed the world. After his retirement, he set about fulfilling a youthful pledge to give away all his money, an aim that, with a final burst near the end, he at last succeeded in doing.

I confess a personal interest in this story. My grandparents fled from rural poverty in Slovakia, then a province of the Austro-Hungarian Empire, to find opportunity in and around the nascent iron and steel industry of western Pennsylvania. I need no persuasion that life was exceedingly hard, and sometimes bitterly unfair, for immigrant workers. But that the opportunity provided to my family by this new industry was superior to anything then available to them in Europe or anywhere else, I also have no doubt. I know they thought so. My maternal grandfather, who had his stint in the steel mills (as also did several of my uncles and cousins on my father's side), never even wanted to talk about the "old country," although he did send contributions back to Matica Slovenska, the national center for Slovak studies.

Carnegie created opportunity, and in the end wealth, for far more families than his own. One of the 1,946 libraries he built in small towns across the United States (he also built 865 in other lands) was a blessing for our family in Johnstown, as was another for my wife's family in Cresco, Iowa, a town of 2,000 inhabitants.

Thank God, I might say, that the good reverends of 1891 did not get their wish: that all creation of wealth should stop, until all existing wealth should be distributed to all, and that those private persons of genius who created wealth should be denied private opportunity to realize their calling, on the grounds that becoming a millionaire was to become a "social monstrosity."

The ignorance of these good clergymen about the system of wealth creation, and their complacence in that ignorance, is staggering. Their preoccupation with the poor is admirable as far as it goes. Yet it is hard to forgive their blindness to crucial facts: to rise out of poverty, the poor need jobs; prospective employees need to find employers; and inventors and originators need to create new industries. Moreover, despite their loathing of inequality, the prospect of personal wealth, however offensive they might find the earning of wealth, is of itself an innocent, if lowly and society-wide, incentive. The desire to better one's condition (and the condition of one's children) is universal, endowed in all by nature. It is a healthy drive and is for all families the inner spring of progress out of poverty. Unless it is present, hope for the poor is bleak.

Moreover, in order to recognize the great contributions that Andrew Carnegie (and others like him) made to moving countless millions in the United States out of their centuries-long poverty, it is not necessary to deny their moral faults. They were not saints. Sometimes, to use old (but still current) theological language, they sinned gravely.

The one episode in his life that Andrew Carnegie was most ashamed of and gave him most pain in memory was the Homestead Steel strike in 1892, which ended in virtual warfare between townspeople (including women and children) and some 300 Pinkerton detectives. Exchanges of gunfire led to nearly a dozen deaths. Only the calling out of the Pennsylvania National Guard and their armed occupation of Homestead restored order (perhaps better, enforced *dis*order, by effectively defending one side, management). Foreseeing the impending conflict, Carnegie left Pittsburgh for his annual trip to Scotland.

In writings and speeches throughout his later life, Andrew Carnegie denied responsibility for the horrible scenes that ensued, although he also refused publicly to blame his management team. His private correspondence, available to scholars only much later, shows that, from far away and behind the scenes, he explicitly cheered his team on. He gave approval in advance to the local manager, Henry Clay Frick, to do whatever it took, using his own judgment, to break the union. This approval flew in the face of every principle about labor that Carnegie had publicly articulated for years and for which he was world famous.

Carnegie's widely propounded principle had always been not to act hastily, never to hire other workers (scabs) to replace strikers, to wait, to listen to them, to reason with them, to reach an acceptable accommodation no matter how long it took. His public view was that well-trained and motivated workers are difficult to replace; it is easier to satisfy a skilled workforce through reasoned negotiation. All this he violated at Homestead. He lived in denial about what he had done, only later confessing how much he regretted it and how much it haunted him. He created an inner cover story to hide his guilt from himself; the pathos is expressed in his *Autobiography*.

In Pittsburgh, Carnegie was widely blamed for his moral cowardice—fleeing to his beloved Scotland before the event took place and, once there, publicly affecting to have been incommunicado. But, of course, he learned of events sometimes within hours, certainly the next day or so. Carnegie went to Scotland for months every year, so this charge hardly bothered him. But he often said that he wished in retrospect that he had stayed home and handled matters according to his stated principles. He deceived himself into thinking that he would have done differently in person than his subordinates did, conveniently masking (even from himself, perhaps) the orders he had given them. He was certainly a moral coward in never owning up to his personal responsibility, not even in private. He did express bitter regrets.

Months afterward, Carnegie went back to Pittsburgh, spoke before the townspeople of Homestead, and in later writings magnified out of all proportion the support a few workers expressed for him personally. He tried to make up in philanthropy for Homestead for the wrong done, building a huge complex that housed a library, auditorium, swimming pool, and gymnasium, and later leaving an endowment to support additional pensions for his workers and for other families in need. Unlike most of his other philanthropies, however, his gifts to

Homestead, grand as they were, carried the attic odor of atonement come too late. Still, it was atonement and to that extent a veiled admission of guilt.

✦

Like all other fields, business is fraught with patches of moral ambiguity, and clear lines between good and evil are difficult to draw. In times of doubt, either a trusted and candid counselor or a conscience striving to be honest is the best guide, especially after prayer for such calm objectivity as human darkness is allowed. Since exact human judgment is often beyond our powers, at times one is grateful that God is our judge. Even great presidents like Abraham Lincoln have learned the strain and anguish of living under the just judgments of God, and trusted in his mercy. They know that moral ambiguity grants them no license, and God's wrathful justice will never be deceived. Words they loved reflect their fear:

> *Mine eyes have seen the Glory*
> *of the coming of the Lord*
> *He has trampled on the vineyards*
> *where the grapes of wrath are stored*
> *He has loosed the fateful lightning*
> *of His terrible swift sword.*

Nihilists, of course, fear no judgment but their own. In their eyes, their deeds are as good as any. Their one "moral" guide is the exercise of their naked will against the nothingness. (But *moral* is for them a forbidden term.) The measure of all things is their own choice. But do nihilists, in fact, escape the grapes of wrath or the terrible swift sword?

Atheists who are not nihilists also know that they are bound by conscience, which they find in their own reason and in the judgment of their fellows down the ages. And if despite their beliefs (since believing does not make things so), there is a God, they expect that reason is in accord with the judgment of God. No one escapes.

The fact that so many in our culture—from so many points of view—have attacked capitalism as immoral, and successful industrialists such as Carnegie as "moral monsters," suggests the opposite of moral relativism. It suggests a fiercely defended worldview, including the existence of an objective moral code or, at least, of objective "laws of history." It embodies, in short, a socialist metaphysics. Sometimes this metaphysics lingers in mind, even after its practical economic experiment has been swept away by history.

The lingering effects of a socialist way of thinking can still be felt in the accusations made against Carnegie by the Reverends Hughes and Tucker. Even if in his activities he had been as innocent as driven snow, their real objection to him would stand: he was part of a wicked system, wicked because it generated inequality such as was exemplified by his own vast accumulation of personal wealth. Their real objection was against the system qua system. Those who think the system wicked will scarcely acquit those whose wealth flows from it, even if they concede that his genius created that wealth where others in the past had not.

The question of the moral structure of the system is unavoidable, and in some ways prior to the question of individual guilt or innocence.

THE MORAL CASE FOR
THE SYSTEM QUA "SYSTEM"

As the sociologist Max Weber (1864–1920) wrote in *The Protestant Ethic and the Spirit of Capitalism*, the assertion that capitalism promotes greed belongs in the kindergarten of sociological opinions. The contrary is true. Where the creation of plenty is the aim, particular material goods lose their high value and become plentiful and cheap. Further, what people have, they again put to risk, reinvesting it. The aim is not acquisition but increase. The clutching fist is not the capitalist style.

Capitalist peoples practice high tolerance for risk. They are open to reality and trust in its essential benevolence, and they respect its rules. In imagination, invention, and investment in the unseen future, business in a capitalist system is unlike business in the past.

Barter and trade are as old as humankind. No one person being self-sufficient (the mythical Robinson Crusoe aside), they are essential to the human condition. What capitalism adds to precapitalist forms of business is a new conception of system. In earlier times, and for many centuries (in Machiavelli's Italy, for example) the main focus of human energy was the acquisition of political power, in order to bring order out of chaos and to add to the rule of law the sanction of authority. In the eighteenth century, a new focus for human energy was suggested by such Scottish thinkers as Adam Ferguson, Francis Hutcheson, David Hume, and Adam Smith.

These champions of civic humanism argued that for common people, it would be better if the aim of social systems ceased being power and plunder. It would be better if the leading social purpose became the pursuit of plenty and the creation of new wealth. In that case, one could hope to banish poverty from all the nations of the earth.

Adam Smith called his new civic aim "universal affluence." In advance of the dread prediction of Thomas Malthus (1766–1834) that the world faced universal impoverishment, famine, and fratricide, Smith raised the banner of the yet-untapped wealth of nations. He was among the first to see the enormous stakes involved in designing a system to accord with the "system of natural liberty," in order to liberate humankind from the prison of poverty and scarcity.

In 1776, the year his groundbreaking book was published, it had not yet entered anyone's head—except Adam Smith's—that something could be done about universal poverty, except by way of compassionate remediation in traditional hospitals, orphanages, almsgiving, and other good works. Most peoples of the world lived by subsistence farming and spent much of the year in idleness. Wars were frequent, and brigands and robbers marauded the lonely roads between towns and villages. On many of these points, the historical essays of David Hume (1711–1776), great friend of Adam Smith, are eloquent.

Smith attached great importance to changing the world's mind about the economic system it was then living under and proposing the outlines of a new system that was already taking shape, through the process of trial and error, all around them. This new system promised, in his eyes, great good for the human race, especially the poor. In fact, the greatest good that inquisitive and ambitious young people could bring the world would be to explain to others the laws of this new system.

Adam Smith was the first to notice, as ancient and medieval writers had not, two natural impulses in every man and woman: the *desire to truck and barter* and the *desire parents feel to better their condition for the sake of their children*. He tried to discern which institutions would allow these two laws to flower. A third law was also implicit in his analysis: the *impulsion of personal economic initiative*. This impulse is the economic expression of natural liberty. Early in his treatise, he used the example of the pin-making machine to point out the coiled dynamism of intellectual discovery, inventiveness, and economic creativity at the base of his new system.

In a great and pregnant passage, Smith called attention to the immense good that springs from a right understanding of this new system qua system. He appealed to the idealism of the young men of Scotland, who gathered in associations and clubs dedicated to social improvement. (Forming such clubs and associations was another of his projects; he believed a vital civil society necessary for a free society.)

> If you would implant public virtue in the breast of him who seems heedless of the interest of his country, it will often be to no purpose to tell him, what superior advantages the subjects of a well-governed state enjoy; that they are better lodged, that they are better clothed, that they are better fed. These considerations will commonly make no great impression.

It's hard not to agree with Smith on that point. Those of us who have tried that line of argument know how it fails. "That's sheerly an appeal to materialism," some will say. Others will say, "Yes, but what have you done for me lately?" Smith goes on:

> You will be more likely to persuade, if you describe *the great system* of public [policy] which procures these advantages, if you explain the connexions and dependencies of its several parts, their mutual subordination to one another, and their general subserviency to the happiness of the society; if you show how this *system* might be introduced into his own country, what it is that hinders it from taking place there at present, how those obstructions might be removed, and all the several wheels of the machine of government be made to move with more harmony and smoothness, without grating upon one another, or mutually retarding one another's motions. It is scarce possible that a man should listen to a discourse of this kind, and not feel himself animated to some degree of public spirit. [Emphasis added.]

Smith held that expositions about how the system works, "if just, and reasonable, and practicable, are of all the works of speculation the most useful." Lectures on such matters "animate the public passions of men, and rouse them to seek out the means of promoting the happiness of the society."

Long ago, Aristotle noted the importance of the architecture of the social system as a whole. Having been born on an

island overrun by invading armies, Aristotle well knew that
even good men are forced under occupation to depart from
earlier ethical standards. The system men live under matters,
especially in their moral lives. Aristotle learned the hard way
that ethics is, for this reason, a branch of politics.

We have seen even in our own time how great changes in
politics—such as the welfare system built in the United States
after 1965—have altered behaviors. Between 1965 and 1995,
births out of wedlock shot up to 30 percent of all births, from
a century-old base of under 5 percent. Something about the
system went wrong. Disquisitions on the system and its laws,
we may well agree with Smith, "are of all works of speculation
the most useful."

I saw this vividly on a trip many years ago to Argentina,
when inflation was running at more than 200 percent per week.
I brought home for my children a note once worth 20 million
in local currency and now worth about one U.S. cent. What
should good parents in Argentina do if they had saved the
equivalent of $10,000 for the higher education of their daugh-
ter? If they invested it in Argentina, its value would dissolve. If
they invested it abroad, economic development in Argentina
would be deprived of capital. Whichever course they chose was
wrong. A bad regime cramps moral space. Under bad systems,
morally good actions are penalized. Good people are pressured
to act less than morally. Thus do bad systems self-destruct.
(Happily for Argentina, the people insisted on radical reform,
and it occurred.)

SINNERS IN THE SYSTEM

Of course, life is no morality play. The good do not always win,
and the wicked often prosper for a long time—and, looking
down their noses, laugh at the "foolishness" of the virtuous.
But even thieves depend on a modicum of honor and trust.

Alas for them, each of their immoral actions sows its own irrationality into the pattern of events, against which others in reaction are obliged to make countermoves. Each immoral act pressures the actions of others to become less than open or efficient. Trust declines; all now proceed guardedly. This, in turn, creates other surds. In this way, rationality slowly unravels until, in the darkness, the war of all against all breaks out. (Consider suspicion in Saddam Hussein's inner circles.)

By contrast, under the rule of law, when human interactions can be more or less open and honest, when trust is a well-established social inheritance, and when the system itself maximizes reasonableness and voluntariness, good people can freely express their own open and good inclinations, and reasoned behavior is rewarded.

Even under well-designed systems, some people will do evil, and good people will sometimes stumble. That is why, under a well-designed system, the worst abuses must be prevented by efficient checks and balances, vigilant media, and an alert public opinion jealous of its moral inheritance. Some social structures promote and then reward virtuous behavior, and punish deviations. Of course, a moral people must avoid becoming so puritan and censorious that a regime of virtue seems excessively intrusive and coercive. Liberality and magnanimity (in the ancient Greek sense of a certain largeness of soul) are needed to make such a regime work.

It is best if moral principles are internalized by citizens, so that they become watchmen over their own behavior, without need of police outside themselves. And what is true for the social system as a whole is also true for subsystems within it, down to the smallest units.

Within firms, for example, business leaders will want to create moral, reasonable, and worker-friendly environments. Cheating, stealing, bullying, lying, harassment, imperviousness to argument, obsessive selfishness, nosiness, evasion of responsibility, cowardice, constant griping, and other moral deficiencies make a place of work unpleasant or even intolerable. By contrast, it turns out that happy environments require the practice of ordinary virtues—kitchen virtues, so to speak, homespun habits—and are destroyed by common, petty vices.

Structures of virtue encourage virtue, but can be frustrated by those whose habits are destructive. Not even a benign system can withstand the grating effect of those whose errant behavior throws irrationality into its smooth workings. But structures that straightforwardly reward the thuggish and the vicious, as in our time both nazism and communism did, have had sudden and cataclysmic ends. No matter how successful they at first appeared, they weakened, shook, and ground to a halt all at once.

Still, they sounded a tocsin that we should not ignore. After seventy years of suffering under communism—even forty years was enough to make many good persons, in jail or under internal banishment, lose heart—some began to believe that the rule of thugs would last forever. It was difficult, day after day, to believe that there really is justice. It was hard to live by justice without even a glimmer of recognition or reward.

Such observations lead one to believe that there are at least a few objective moral laws that cannot be violated without eventual self-destruction. Certainly you can violate them, for you are free, but you—and others—will pay. For a long time, the unjust and the evil-minded flourish, while the just are plagued by unwanted doubts. Often people must cling to virtue for its own sake, without hope of enjoying its usual social benefits, even while enduring the gloating of the unjust. This feature of goodness, in fact, is why we honor it so; were good acts always rewarded, we might think them simply self-interested, even calculated, rather than noble.

It remains true that good and morally admirable people make work environments, friendships, and even cities and nations happy places in which to find oneself, for which one gives thanks; whereas the company of vicious people is no fun at all, unless you are one of them.

The human condition is such that not all people are good, even middling good. Some are extremely weak and unreliable, and others, for whatever reasons, are just plain evil. In the general case, every one of us sometimes does what we know we ought not to do, and does not do what we know we ought to do. Each of us, in the old-fashioned word, sometimes sins. This fact about human beings places any workable human system under severe constraints.

No wise social system is designed to be peopled only by saints; there are not enough saints to people a whole system. (And the few there are can be at times impossible to live with.)

Thus, a workable human system—especially a system of political economy that must harness the passions of the willful, the passionate, and even the unscrupulous—cannot be designed solely for saints. It must allow for the faults, sometimes serious faults and self-delusions, of all of us. It must have plenty of checks and balances. It needs to divide every major form of power and to place different forms of power in different hands, so that each power may be a sentinel over the other.

A wise system needs to supply remedies for the moral defects of all. When errors in direction are spotted, hopefully in timely fashion, it relies on mechanisms of self-reform and self-correction. It needs to diffuse as widely as possible the powers of decision making. It needs to recognize the dignity and creative capacity of every person.

This is a lot for a human system to encompass. For such reasons, a design that comes closest to what is desired is most likely to grow out of human experience, by trial and error. It is not at all likely to spring from a pure, clear, and distinct concept reached by a committee. In our time, most designs of utopia arrived at by committee have ended up murderous.

Wisdom learned the hard way, through centuries of experience, is likely to be best.

WRONG ABOUT CAPITALISM

Some highly successful businesspeople, like that early one, Andrew Carnegie, do not well grasp the architecture of the free society. Ironically, Carnegie understood the democratic part and misunderstood the capitalist part. A great defender of the republican form of government and a great foe of monarchy, Carnegie showed an immigrant's gratitude to America in his eloquent book of 1886, *Triumphant Democracy*, a best-seller in the United States and Britain. The book contains many wonderful insights. Carnegie held that a democracy should often regulate business in ways that business needs but cannot establish for itself and that business has many obligations to the civil order in which it prospers.

Nonetheless, Carnegie was too much under the influence of his friend Herbert Spencer, the famous Darwinian social scientist, to grasp the real kernel of capitalism. This may seem ironic, but it is true. As artists are not necessarily the best interpreters of their own work, so practitioners in many fields do not need to know the theory of what they are doing and, if asked, state it badly—maybe even in the wrong key.

During his lifetime, Carnegie was attacked for writing that at a higher stage of economic organization, the rise of a few rich persons with a large surplus of wealth is "inevitable." The Reverend Tucker argued that St. Matthew never said, "The rich ye shall always have with ye," as in the gospel according to "St. Andrew," but the *poor*. The reverend thought that Carnegie was dodging moral responsibility by taking refuge in determinism. Indeed, Carnegie erred by employing pseudo-scientific jargon to express simple observations from his own experience, and especially such phrases as the "survival of the fittest," for many ministers were attacking Darwinism during just those years. The Darwinian phrase "survival of the fittest," they said for example, is tautological. How does one recognize the "fittest" except that it has survived? Meanwhile, creatures more beautiful, more excellent, and more precious, but perhaps more fragile, perish easily. Does this mean that the Darwinian mantra ought to be the "survival of the crudest"?

Such criticism did not much bother Carnegie. What he had in mind, what he knew from experience, is that the factory system of modern production led to goods of better quality more cheaply priced and more widely dispersed throughout the population than ever before. He knew this because his firms had invented many new goods with heretofore unimagined possibilities. For example, they invented new types of iron and steel fittings that made possible bridges such as the one that spanned the Mississippi at St. Louis; beams that made possible skyscrapers in cities; steel sheeting for oceangoing vessels; hardened steel for much longer-lasting and better-wearing railroad tracks; and multiple possibilities for new types of train cars and automobiles such as the world had never seen or even dreamed of.

More than that, Carnegie had come to understand that the number of persons who could lead such firms as his—who had the inventiveness, the practical bent, the administrative and managerial skills, and the skills of cost accounting—were exceedingly rare and difficult to find. Identifying them and motivating them, he thought, was his own special talent, the chief secret to his unparalleled success.

Further, Carnegie found the best way to motivate these persons of unusual talent: in lieu of high salaries, he offered them an interest in the business. If he had thought of business as a zero-sum game—whatever one gains, the other loses—he would have been hurting his own interests. But, of course, he thought of it as a win-win game. The more that different talents made the pie grow, the more each would gain.

Further, Carnegie persuaded his associates to deny themselves the premature cashing in of profits, in order to plough everything back into the growth of capital. He preached against greed, in favor of self-restraint. He opposed immediate gratification, in favor of a greater return in the future—a return that would come only if the risks that all were taking vindicated their faith in the social contribution they were making.

Thus, it was by no means inevitable that Carnegie and his top associates would become rich. In fact, not a few of them along the way insisted on taking high wages rather than an interest in the firm, or in selling off their interest for immediate profit. Some preferred a bird in the hand. Some were risk averse. Some did not trust or want to work with some of the other partners. All these lived to regret not following Carnegie's advice.

Those who contained their desires in order to follow his advice stood to lose everything if, as so often happened to other firms, theirs went bust, and their interests in it came to nothing. Carnegie certainly did not mean "inevitable" in the way the Reverend Tucker thought.

Elsewhere in American literature, the great industrialists and financiers who did much to inaugurate the prosperity that transformed the poor of the nineteenth century into the affluent suburbanites of the twentieth century have often been described, in the spirit of Reverend Tucker, as robber barons. Actually, though, none of them—not Carnegie, or Frick, or Rockefeller, Morgan, Harriman, Stillman, Vanderbilt, Mellon, or any of those others usually linked together—was born an aristocrat. Nearly all were born poor. A president of the United States—rather more of an aristocrat himself, T. R. Roosevelt—called them "malefactors of great wealth." The biographer of Henry Clay Frick, benefactor of the Frick Gallery, writes that these "money-makers lived by the gospel of greed."

One should not use the word *greed* carelessly. Many dukes and barons of old did indeed march out with their armies nearly every season, seeking plunder, booty, fame, and power for themselves. Many centuries came and went under their tutelage, with no basic change in the social status of the poor at all. (How much did conditions for the poor actually change in Europe from the year 1250 to Victor Hugo's Paris rebellion of 1831?)

By contrast, the genius and labors of the so-called robber barons of the late nineteenth century transformed social possibilities, dramatically increased social knowledge and social wealth, and set the lives of millions (including most readers of this book) on an upward path.

What they built was built not merely for themselves. They left behind great institutions that have been socially productive for generations after their deaths. These men did more than make money; calling them "money-makers" trivializes what they accomplished. Nor does the word *greed* capture their state of soul. They were not stingy misers, clutching gold coins to their breast, hoarders of gains, petty and avaricious, and closed minded. They were hugely ambitious, creative, sometimes vain, tough, and even ruthless at times—"masters of all honorable tricks" (as Matthew Josephson called Frick)—and certainly not saints. Some of them sometimes behaved wickedly in public or in private. The attempt to understand them under the heading "greed" reveals both historical amnesia and ideological distortion.

"Greed" does not explain why Andrew Carnegie gave virtually all his money away, according to a vow he made long before he gained it; or why, as he was gaining it, he did not take it, keep it, hoard it, or spend it. Instead, he poured it back into his firm as an investment in its future. In other words, he put it at risk. "Greed" is for the impoverished socialist imagination a term of art; its purpose is neither descriptive nor analytical. Its purpose is moral denunciation, for ideological reasons.

Still, if his critics got things wrong, so did Carnegie. His description of the four principles of capitalism as he thought of them—"Individualism, Private Property, the Law of Accumulation of Wealth, and the Law of Competition"—

leaves out other even more crucial principles. His four principles alone do not produce new wealth. His list omits at least two crucial factors: the *creativity* of Carnegie and his associates in almost every sphere of their endeavors, and the new type of *community* he built both among his partners and throughout his far-flung organization.

Without the sense of pride carefully instilled in his workers ("God! We made great steel!" one of his workers said at Homestead years later. "We were the best in the world!") and the deeply and tragically flawed community he encouraged them to form at work; without openness to change and alertness to realities undiscerned by others; and without a broad picture of future trends in the world, Carnegie could not have built what he built, or done what he did. The intellectual dimensions demanded by a capitalist system are almost wholly left out of his account. It is as if, in explaining the system, he had put on the sort of materialist blinders implicit in vulgar Social Darwinism.

In this, Carnegie was no doubt encouraged by the intellectual company he kept, for he loved to spend his free time—several months of every year—in conversation with writers, professors, and artists, and at such times, he avoided the company of other businessmen. He counted among his favorite friends Matthew Arnold, Herbert Spencer, Rudyard Kipling, Mark Twain, John Morley of Oxford, and many others. His views were not untypical for his time and participated in many common misperceptions.

Nonetheless, there is one idea that was unique to Andrew Carnegie: it is a disgrace for an accumulator of great capital to die without giving it all away. He did not believe in bequeathing it, or at least much of it, to one's own family. He thought inherited wealth likely to hurt, rather than to help, the young. In his famous two-part article, "Wealth," his main point was that a rich man should give away all his money—wisely—within his own lifetime if at all possible. He should give it to help persons born poor to overcome their poverty, through the industrious use of their own talents.

In the latter part of his essay, Carnegie elaborated his own carefully considered views about how that may best be done. In chapter 10, we shall return to the problem of the stewardship of wealth and how to do more good than harm with it. Our need now is to gain a fuller understanding of the nature of the system of political economy, within which the calling of business is today being pursued by Christian, Muslim, Jewish, and humanist men and women—and in larger numbers than are engaged in any other calling.

Since it means a great deal for the poor of the world and for the future of democracy, it is to that larger, systemic aspect of business as a vocation to which we now turn. What is it that the world expects from business or, more exactly, from the system of which it is a part, from capitalism? For a century and a half that term, *capitalism*, has been assaulted from left and right, by agrarians and socialists, by distributists and communists, by traditionalists and futurists, by aristocrats and proletarians, by literary figures and sociologists. Get used to it. Having business as a vocation is to gain no esteem from literary elites.

For your own satisfaction, however (and to answer the questions of your children, who may well be hostage to anticapitalist professors), you might wish to recall what Jerry Rubin's wife told the Associated Press (December 2, 1994): "Some say he sold out, but Jerry was willing to have the courage to evolve. . . . He realized that capitalism is the greatest system on earth. He helped many, many people make money and good lives."

For many of us, Jerry Rubin is no authority, and his wife's statement sounds a little too enthusiastic. Nonetheless, think carefully about why yours is an important—no, an indispensable—vocation. I hope the following reflections stimulate you to put it better yourself.

Chapter Four

✦

FOR THE POOR AND
FOR DEMOCRACY

For development to take root, private property, contractual obligations, savings, fair pricing, and security of goods and life must be respected. When individuals are threatened by their own governments, they try to shield themselves from exaction, violence, and corruption by falling back on their own meager resources for subsistence and do not make the slightest effort to produce for posterity. That both Korea and Taiwan are now moving toward greater political plurality illustrates how development leads to the creation of middle classes who aspire to a greater degree of participation in the political process. In the long run, democracy, law, and development intermingle, for all three are based on a universal system of moral values.

—*Guy Sorman*

ONE CHEER IS QUITE ENOUGH

Democracy, Winston Churchill once said, is a bad system of government, except when compared to all the others. Much the same might be said of capitalism. It is not a system much celebrated by poets, philosophers, and priests. From time to time, it has seemed romantic to the young, but not very often. Capitalism is a system that commends itself best to the middle-aged, after they have gained some experience of the way history treats the plans of men. In order to be grateful for capitalism, one does not have to indulge in excessive celebration.

My own fields of inquiry are theology and philosophy. From the perspective of these fields, I would not want it to be thought that any system on earth is the Kingdom of God. Capitalism isn't. Democracy isn't. The two combined are not. The best that can be said for them (and it is quite enough) is that, in combination, capitalism, democracy, and pluralism are more protective of the rights, opportunities, and conscience of ordinary citizens—all citizens—than any known alternative.

Many people in this world seem not to be satisfied except by utopian thinking. In America, thank God, since at least *The Federalist* No. 10, our people have resisted the "utopic theorists." We prefer a practical philosophy that works, especially one that works better than any known alternative. We have in mind certain ideals, of course. In their light, we form criteria for judging what works better and what works worse. And we insist on keeping actual working models under the judgment of ideals. Fortunately, however, we do not confuse ideals with the messy models that work. We try hard not to allow the perfect to become the enemy of the good. We prefer imperfect real things to perfect nonexistents.

BUT WHAT IS "CAPITALISM"?

It's a dirty trick to play on a reader, I know, but this is the time to ask you to raise your eyes from this book a moment and attempt to define capitalism. Ask yourself now, "What is capitalism?" and take five minutes to satisfy yourself that you have a defensible answer. If you are like most people I have asked this question of over the past fifteen years, you will hesitate, take a stab at it, and cover your ego by saying something like, "I know what capitalism is, but I can't define it."

Don't feel alone.

In human history, capitalism is a new system. Max Weber held that it arose only some generations after the Protestant Reformation, though it had earlier precursors. R. H. Tawney also thought of capitalism as a late arrival. In my view, both of these thinkers, and many others, misjudged the essence of capitalism, but they are no doubt correct in thinking that the new term *capitalism* applies only to a system that appeared during the past two hundred years.

In 1848, Karl Marx marveled at the newness and the greatness of this new thing: "The bourgeoisie, during its rule of scarce 100 years, has created more massive and more colossal productive forces than of all preceding generations together." In 1848, he hadn't seen the half of it!

Most readers are not likely to realize that Karl Marx gave capitalism—the system he hated fiercely—its now-classic definition, one repeated, in slightly different words, in seven different English-language dictionaries I've consulted. They all mention three elements: a system of market exchange, private property, and private accumulation or profit. Knowing Marx's animosity against capitalism, why should we accept that definition? It is contrary to the empirical evidence.

Markets, private property, and profit were already present in biblical times. Beginning in about 1750, a critical mass of institutions (some new, some old) began to coalesce in a new way. The reason that a new word such as *capitalism* was needed (it was first used about 1810) was to name a new thing—a new ingredient that transformed the ancient, sleepy marketplace into a dynamic search for new goods, services, methods, and processes. As Max Weber and many other historians of economics have noted, a new kind of economic system emerged during the late eighteenth century.

Economists are still divided on what that new thing is. My own view, following Joseph Schumpeter, Friedrich Hayek, and Israel Kirzner, but in my own words, is as follows: Capitalism is an economic system, dependent on an appropriate political system and a supportive moral-cultural system, that unites a large variety of social institutions (some new, some old) in the support of human economic creativity. It is the system oriented to the human mind: *caput* (L. "head"), wit, invention, discovery, enterprise. It brings institutional support to the inalienable right to personal economic initiative.

An economic system constituted by relatively free markets and a regime of private property is not necessarily capitalist. Most societies from the ancient world to today display those characteristics. To take but one example, Jerusalem during the biblical period was hardly anything but a market. It was neither an industrial nor an agricultural center. It was a marketplace at the crossroads of three continents. It was also a regime of private property. Otherwise, the commandment, "Thou shalt not steal," would have seemed pointless. Yet it would be odd, and quite mistaken, to describe biblical Jerusalem as capitalist.

Consider another example. Suppose that after the collapse of socialism in 1989, the Polish Zehm (parliament) passed legislation doing away with price fixing by a central planning agency, in order to permit prices to be set by markets. Suppose, too, that it reinstated and strengthened laws protecting rights to private property, as well as the private accumulation of economic gains from the sale or use of property. Suppose, finally, that the people of Poland, after the passage of such laws, remained as passive as they had been taught to be under communism, and did virtually nothing—while waiting for the government to do something else.

Would laws establishing rights to market activity, private property, and private profit result in a new—capitalist—system? Not by themselves. The crucial element is an outbreak of personal economic enterprise. It was only in 1990, when 500,000 Poles showed the economic activism to start new businesses, and another 1 million during 1991, that one could say that a new spirit was at last infusing the new Polish framework, a new virtue of enterprise was coming to life, and something like capitalism was at last stirring, like seedlings in spring.

What is the virtue of enterprise? Like any other virtue, it is a habit or disposition—in this case, a disposition of both the intellect and the will. It is a disposition, first, to notice, to gain an insight into, to discover something that others unseeingly pass by. It is a disposition, second, to choose to take a risk— well before one in twenty of the factors necessary to generate success are known—and to begin making happen what the agent sees as at least a possibility. Enterprise further requires the habitual courage necessary to realize a dream. It is, first, a dream and then the determined, persistent, and self-correcting process of making it real.

In *The Spirit of Enterprise* (one of the best books on the practitioners of business ever written), George Gilder contrasts the habit of enterprise with the bureaucratic, established habits of the already successful. Enterprise, he writes, "is the creation of surprises." It entails breaking the glass walls of established ideas. It does not proceed by mastery of the particulars of existing ideas but by stepping out into the unknown to create new realities to which *others* must react. Enterprise is an "aggressive action, not a reaction"; it forces others—other businesses, labor, government—to react to it. It is forever making the world new.

R. H. Tawney, the British socialist historian, interpreted the "new thing" in capitalism as acquisitiveness or greed. But these are not new; they are as old as Midas. Besides, greed is not a creative passion. Like the other deadly vices, it introduces irrationality into everything it touches. Greed is such a stupid vice that it unravels rationality in others, who are baffled by its presence. How can an intelligent person harbor it? How can anyone deal with a blindness so banal?

Gilder lists people who built great businesses through sheer creative flair in dealing with dirty, gritty problems. One of them, the founder of Browning-Ferris Industries, Thomas J. Fatjo, gained key insights into waste management from hauling bags of garbage in his own hands in the hot streets of Houston. Another, the founder of a great food-processing company, gained his key insight while sorting potatoes tediously by hand in a dark warehouse. A third, a key contributor to Micron's 64K dynamic random access memory, gained his from years of menial drawing of layout patterns in the back rooms of his firm. Gilder asserts that this is also true of thousands of other founders of businesses: those who have done the dirty work at the bottom often have the best chance of gaining the crucial insight that overturns existing establishments. The executives at the top are too busy trying to keep the old ways humming.

Gilder even tips his cap to Andrew Carnegie, who never claimed to know all the technologies of steel production: "Carnegie's real enterprise was not steel but industrial combination." Carnegie was a genius at putting things together, and especially at gathering around him "men who were more clever than himself."

Otherwise pompous, like some other uncommonly short men, Carnegie "was humble enough to listen" to voices from inside the heart of the mills and in the back rooms of the accountants. He was always on the lookout for real knowledge and unusual talent. For entrepreneurs, "the first law is to listen. They must be meek enough—and shrewd enough—to endure the humbling eclipse of self that comes in the process of profound learning from others." True creators have a passionate love for learning; they thirst to get reality straight and true. They want what they create to endure. They want it to withstand the buffetings of wind and sea, like a spray-drenched vessel "built to last."

Capitalism is a 200-year-old system constituted by sets of institutions and practices that allow women and men of creative talent to find cheap legal incorporation, liability protection, venture capital, financial instruments, patent and copyright protection, open entry into markets, favorable tax and regulatory policies, analytic tools, bookkeeping practices, and other necessary instruments for making their dreams become reality.

But the *heart* of capitalism is not constituted by these formal instruments. It is constituted, rather, by creative wit and the sheer joy of creating something solid, substantial, lasting, and worth losing one's shirt for. The zest is in the creating. The money that may (or may not) follow is more akin to public recognition than it is end in itself; it arrives like justice earned. To most creators, the money itself is boring. If you don't believe me, watch them. They prefer new risks and challenges. When these wither, they wither.

CAPITALISM IS BETTER FOR THE POOR

There are two powerful arguments in favor of capitalism over its historical alternatives: (1) capitalism better helps the poor to escape from poverty than any other system and (2) capitalism is a necessary condition for the success of democracy. Before coming to those arguments, though, a discussion of the alternatives may be useful.

On this planet today, there are only two real alternatives to capitalism: socialism, found in North Korea, Cuba, Vietnam, the Republic of China, and a few other places; and the traditional third world state-controlled economy, found in much of Latin America, most of Africa, and large sections of Asia.

Some people would add that social democracies, such as Germany and the Scandinavian countries, are a third alternative. It seems more accurate to say that such forms of social democracy are part of a continuum with democratic capitalism, though they are quite far toward the leftward extreme of state control. This is how the sociologist Peter Berger analyzes the data in *The Capitalist Revolution*. One piece of evidence for his point is that leading socialists in such countries describe their systems as "rotten, corrupt, bourgeois, capitalist countries" (which they are trying to whip into the shape of true socialist societies). If the socialists call these nations "capitalist," that's good enough for me.

I offer, then, two propositions, to whose truth much powerful evidence attests. First, better than the third world economies and better than the socialist economies, capitalism makes it possible for the vast majority of the poor to break out of the prison of poverty; to find opportunity; to discover full scope for their own personal economic initiative; and to rise into the middle class and higher. Watch the crowds on the streets of free nations: they walk the walk of the free—erect and purposeful and quick.

To repeat: Capitalism is better for the poor than is socialism or the traditional third world economy. Sound evidence for this proposition is found in the migration patterns of the poor of the world. From which countries do they emigrate, and to which countries do they go? Overwhelmingly they flee from socialist and third world countries, and they line up at the doors of the capitalist countries, often in long lines curving around the corner like theater-goers queuing for a Broadway hit.

A second way of bringing sound evidence to light is to ask of virtually any audience, in almost any capitalist country, how many generations back in family history they have to go before they reach poverty. For the vast majority of us in the United States, we need go back no further than our parents or our grandparents. In 1900, a large plurality of Americans lived (as the world went) in comfortable rural poverty. Their living conditions, however mean, were still better than those of virtually all other world populations (hence the tide of immigrants to these shores). Still, by today's standards, both their rural comfort and their urban immigrant settlements in the crowded cities were barely higher than subsistence. They were poor. Yet most of these same families today are described as affluent. Capitalist systems *have* raised up the poor; we know this from our own families. We *remember* poverty.

Let me make this point another way. In the year 1800, demographers estimate that there were only 750 million people on earth. Some calculate that the average age at death was then about eighteen. Just 196 years later, in 1996, thanks largely to new discoveries in such fields as sanitation and hygiene, medicine and pharmaceuticals, the number of living humans surpassed 5.5 billion, and the average age at death has risen to more than fifty-eight even in the poorest nations, and to over seventy-five in the advanced nations. Because more people live longer, more are alive at this moment—and their material conditions are far better than those of 200 years ago. A tiny example: Most of this nation's founders had some wooden teeth, and George Washington was bled to death by his physician.

I have heard the argument that most of these people are alive today because of technology, not capitalism. But whence came the drive to advance technology—and not only through gaining knowledge about it, but by bringing it to markets that carry it to billions of individuals—if not from an enterprising, dynamic market system?

How many pharmaceuticals do you have in your home that were developed in communist countries or, for that matter, in third world countries, even *rich* third world countries (rich, that is, in natural endowments, such as Saudi Arabia and Brazil, Colombia, Indonesia, and Nigeria)?

Enterprising firms striving to bring one discovery after

another to market learn by experience how to spot still other technological possibilities. Over the years, they acquired the practical know-how to bring these possibilities to market in the most desirable and cheapest forms they could. If they did not do so, they knew their competitors—actual or potential—would.

The former Soviet Union trained possibly the largest body of scientists and technical experts ever assembled in history. Yet all these brains brought pitifully little of the knowledge they acquired into the common service of humanity. They had little incentive—and no market system—to enable them to do so. So far as the common people experience, knowledge apart from marketing systems stands idle and out of service, like a broken-down bus.

A NECESSARY CONDITION FOR DEMOCRACY

The second great argument is that capitalism is a necessary condition for the success of democracy but not a sufficient condition. This is an empirical proposition, based on cases that have already appeared before our eyes. There have been countries that are (or were) capitalist but not democratic. The fact that a country is capitalist is not a sufficient condition for its becoming democratic. Nonetheless, the instances of Greece, Portugal, Spain, Chile (after Pinochet), South Korea, and others allow us to predict that once a capitalist system has generated a sufficiently large and successful middle class, the pressures turning it toward democracy grow very strong. This is because successful entrepreneurs soon acquire evidence that they are smarter and more able than generals and commissars. They begin demanding self-government. As has been recognized since ancient times, the middle class is the seedbed of the republican spirit.

In both democracy and capitalism, the rule of law is crucial. In both, limited government is crucial. In both, the protection of the rights of individuals and minorities is crucial.

Although capitalism and democracy do not necessarily go together, at least in the world of theory, in the actual world of concrete historical events, they are led toward an almost predestined marriage, both by their inner dynamism and by their instinct for survival. "Capitalism" and "democracy" go together as "political" and "economy." The "system of natural liberty" naturally seeks expression in both politics and economics, in republican forms of government and capitalist forms of economy.

On this basis, one can predict that as the entrepreneurial spirit grows in the People's Republic of China, particularly in its southern provinces, and as the Chinese middle class gains in self-confidence and independence, an ever-rising tide in favor of democratic institutions will slap against the sides of the governmental structures of China. The free economy will unleash forces that propel China toward the free polity.

A NECESSARY CONDITION FOR CAPITALISM

For a moment allow me to stress the other side of this proposition. Some dictators have chosen to permit capitalist systems to function within their borders, although such systems put a severe limitation on their own personal power over the economy. Nonetheless, a double defect inherent in one-man rule makes capitalism in such nations vulnerable: human mortality and the problem of succession it entails. Dictatorships face intractable and treacherous perplexities in solving the problem of succession. One of the great advantages of democracy is that it solves that problem in a routine, regular, and peaceful way. For the long-term health of capitalism, then, I venture the hypothesis that democracy, with its methods of peaceful succession, is also a necessary condition.

That is not the only support for my hypothesis. Another service to capitalism that democracy performs better than dictatorship derives from its representational function. A free economy has a great many parts, and a representative parliament tends to represent all these parts. In a democracy, every part of the economy has at least some active voice. This may make it more difficult for clear and simple decisions to be made, and it may increase the probabilities of one form or another of gridlock. But the active representation of all economic parties does make less likely the harsh, unilateral decisions to which dictators are prone, which have the potential of wiping out entire sections of the economy with one false move.

Democratic rulers are forced to face all the consequences of their decisions. Dictators are not. Pinochet and other dictators have caused great harm to their economies by unconsidered, unilateral decisions, which a parliament might have prevented them from making.

Thus, the obverse of the main proposition seems also to be true: democracy seems as necessary (but not sufficient) for successful long-term capitalism as capitalism is necessary (but not sufficient) for the success of democracy.

Let us return to the main argument. In Eastern Europe today and, in general, around the world, people will not love democracy if it does not bring improvement in their economic conditions. They will not be satisfied with democracy if all it means is the opportunity to vote every two years. They want to see economic conditions improve.

Typically people do not ask for utopia, but they would like to see the possibility of solid economic progress for their families over the next three or four years. They want at least some small improvements, and they need a realistic hope that those will actually happen. This is the psychological mechanism that makes capitalism, or at least a dynamic economy, indispensable to the success of democracy. Capitalism delivers the goods that democracy holds out as one of its promises.

CAPITALISM REDUCES ENVY

> Commerce is a cure for the most destructive prejudices;
> for it is almost a general rule, that wherever we find
> agreeable manners, there commerce flourishes; and that
> wherever there is commerce, there we meet with agree-
> able manners.
>
> ————*Montesquieu*

Another service provided by capitalism to democracy is less well understood. The founders of the United States understood it very clearly, however, as one can see by a careful study of *The Federalist* Nos. 10 and 51. Benjamin Franklin in London and Thomas Jefferson in Paris searched libraries to find out why virtually all previous republics had failed, often in a single generation.

During a lecture in Washington several years ago, Lady Thatcher congratulated Americans for preserving the world's oldest republican government. It is hard to build a republic that lasts, she said, and added a humorous anecdote to illustrate the point. An Englishman in the country visited his local library to request a copy of the constitution of the French Republic. The librarian peered at him over her glasses and replied, not at all apologetically, "My dear, we don't carry periodicals."

But why do republics so regularly fall? Which passion kills them? Envy, it turns out, is the most destructive social passion—more so than hatred. Hatred is at least visible and universally recognized as evil. Envy seldom operates under its own name. It chooses a lovelier name to hide behind and prefers to do its work invisibly.

In virtually all earlier republics, envy set class against class, sections of cities against other sections, leading family against leading family. For this reason, the early Americans stood against division ("Divided we fall") and sought ways to neutralize envy. Unless a republic defeats envy, it cannot stand.

Thinking carefully, step by step, our founders determined

that a lasting republic could not be built on the clerical or priestly class or on the aristocracy and military classes, whose sense of "honor" had led to many rivalries and wars. A lasting republic would have to be built—could only be built—on a far humbler and widely despised class. Thus, our founders opted for what they called a "commercial republic." (My own phrase, "democratic capitalism," which I wish I had copyrighted, is intended to be a contemporary expression of that term.)

Why did the founders choose as their social foundation a class, and an activity, universally regarded by philosophers, religious leaders, and poets as lowly and ignoble? Why did they choose crass commerce? Lowly, servile, mercantile industry? Things instrumental rather than those ends in themselves that the liberal arts have always held to be superior, as the noble is superior to the ignoble?

They chose the humbler path for two reasons. First, when every person in the republic, especially the able-bodied poor, sees that his or her material conditions are improving from year to year, they are led to compare where they are today with where they would like to be tomorrow. They stop comparing themselves with their neighbors, because their personal goals are not the same as those of their neighbors. They seek their own goals, at their own pace, to their own satisfaction.

Indeed, in America, as Tocqueville and others noted, there was a remarkable freedom from envy. On the whole, people rejoiced in the success of their neighbors, as tokens of the coming prosperity of their village, city, and nation. Across America today, in public schools and colleges and universities, one still sees many portraits of those who were successful in commerce and industry, honored as public benefactors. Democracy depends on a growing economy for its upward tide—for social mobility, opportunity, and the pursuit of personal accomplishment.

Consider how this works in practice. Two sisters born in Nebraska travel to New York to find careers. As it happens, not without heartbreaks along the way, neither sister marries, but both find good jobs. Alice, the older one, retains the thrifty habits of her Nebraska childhood, lives nicely, and steadily puts aside significant sums every year. She invests in a growth fund (one-third) and a blue chip mutual fund (two-thirds), considering herself a little more modern and adventuresome than her father, who went through World War I and the Great Depression.

Meanwhile, her sister Sarah thinks Alice is crazy. "You don't have any children. What are you saving for? You should live a little," she tells Alice often—too often. Sarah spends everything she has. She loves eating out, wearing fine clothes, furnishing her apartment expensively. Her passion is travel. She has been to the Himalayas, to Constantinople, to the Upper Congo, to India, to Australia. The only thing she saves for is for travel— an account she then drains at least every other year for another fabulous trip. She likes going alone, her own way. She knows what she enjoys and plans for a certain degree of luxury, allowing time and space for surprise and adventure.

By the time they reach their sixties, Alice, it turns out, has over a million dollars in her mutual funds (not counting her generous pension, from work). Sarah has no more than $5,000 in all her accounts put together, including her kitchen piggy bank. Do these sisters envy one another? On the contrary. They feel sorry for one another. Each thinks the other is crazy.

Only a liberal sociologist is left to argue that this is an unfair nation, because of the inequitable distribution of wealth demonstrated in cases like this, in which one person has two hundred times more wealth than another.

THE TYRANNY OF A MAJORITY

The second reason the framers chose commerce and industry as the economic foundation for this nation is to defeat another great threat to republican institutions: the tyranny of a majority. Majorities can be even more tyrannical and more cruel than a single dictator. Madison and Hamilton, in particular, understood the ravages of original sin in human affairs. They therefore strongly supported Montesquieu's (and Aquinas's) notion of separated powers. Further, they found a similar "principle of division" throughout every branch of society. The aim in every case was to divide one source of power from another, in such a way that each, in watching out for its own prerogatives, would be a sentinel over the others. Thus, it is easy to see why a republic built on commerce—the commercial republic—commended itself to the practical common sense of our non-utopian forebears.

It is in the nature of commerce and industry that they focus the interests of citizens in many different directions: some in finance, some in production, some in supply, some in wholesale, some in retail, some in transport, some in lumber, others in tobacco, or cotton, or vegetables, or cattle, or sheep, or iron and steel, or coal, or whaling, or glassmaking, or woodwork, or silver and pewter, and the like. In their structure and goals, industry differs from industry, firm from firm. In such ways, commerce and industry render highly unlikely any single, universal economic majority.

In summary, commerce and industry are a necessary condition for the success of republican government ("government of the people, by the people, and for the people") because they (1) defeat envy, through open economic opportunity and economic growth, and (2) defeat the tyranny of a majority, through splitting up economic interests into many different factions.

NATURAL LIBERTY—POLITICAL AND ECONOMIC

What did capitalism promise? First of all, it promised continued improvement in the material conditions of all its citizens, a promise without precedent in human history. Second, it promised an equally unprecedented measure of individual freedom for all of these same citizens.

> And lastly, it held out the promise that, amidst this pros-
> perity and liberty, the individual could satisfy his instinct
> for self-preservation—for leading a virtuous life that sat-
> isfied the demands of his spirit (or as one used to say, his
> soul)—and that the free exercise of such individual
> virtue would aggregate into a just society.
>
> —*Irving Kristol*

Better for the poor and better for democracy: this is the tribute that historical experience pays to capitalism at the end of the twentieth century.

Yet capitalism alone is not the sum of our hopes. Its political expression, as we have seen, is not complete without democracy—or, more exactly, a republican form of government. The latter is characterized by the rule of law; institutional and popular protection for the rights of individuals and minorities; checks against the tyranny of a majority; representative government as a check against popular majorities; the separation of powers; and other remedies for the defects of democracy and the weaknesses of human nature.

The system of natural liberty requires, in other words, both political and economic articulation. But what else? It also requires a moral and cultural system—a regime of virtue, in a modern if not a classical sense. It requires open institutions, but not for that reason empty heads or empty souls. The point of a democratic capitalist system is to serve each person in the whole range of human responsibilities: moral and religious, political and economic.

To protect the rule of law and to secure individual rights, the political order has priority over the economic order. The moral-cultural order has priority over both. Economics is not the be-all and the end-all; it is an instrumental art. But what an instrument!

MORAL VIGILANCE

Capitalism is the best hope for the poor of the third world. It is the necessary condition for the emergence of democracy. It is such a humble thing, but so important.

If it fails—in Central Europe, along that arrow that points out along the huge plain stretching from Poland through Ukraine, on to Belorussia and Russia, and on out to northern Asia—the history of the twenty-first century may be bloodier than the twentieth. Liberty does not come with a guarantee. Its price, our founders reminded us, is everlasting vigilance. Liberty is in some ways the least stable of regimes; it depends on fidelity to key ideas. Any one generation at any moment may surrender liberty, give up on it, thrust it back to the giver.

It could even be that liberty will shortly burn out, having sped like a comet across history for a little more than two centuries, and leave in its wake only darkness. Our future could be bleak.

Such a fate, however, is not commanded by the stars. The greatest threat to liberty lies in the human heart. If our minds cling firmly to basic ideas and if our wills choose what we ought to choose, we still have a chance to make liberty prevail. We have a chance at bat. That's all that free women and free men ask: a chance, not a guarantee.

Still, is capitalism good for the inner life of its own citizens? Does it make them more—or less—virtuous? Ever since socialism proved to be an economic failure, most criticisms of capitalism swarm around a moral charge, "Well, it may be good for the bottom line. But it is spiritually empty and corrosive of virtue."

That is why we must turn next to the moral ecology on which a capitalist system depends. That, in turn, brings to center-stage those ancient pivotal concepts, character and virtue.

Chapter Five

✧

VIRTUE IN THE MODERN CITY

Sow a thought and you reap an act;
Sow an act and you reap a habit;
Sow a habit and you reap a character;
Sow a character and you reap a destiny.
—Anonymous

Even some friends of capitalism, such as the great British historian Paul Johnson, think that it is morally neutral. They point out that its techniques are adaptable to thoroughly different moral cultures, from Japan to France. Other thinkers, of course, believe that although capitalism has some good points, such as efficiency and wealth production, it is infecting the world with materialistic banality.

Reality seems to show, by contrast, that capitalism depends on *human* capital most of all, including the human capital constituted by virtuous habits. A friend of mine from the former Soviet Union reports that by the end of 1995, many Russians had concluded that capitalism is "too strenuous." They liked it better when "everyone was equal and everyone had a job." Under socialism, they had little liberty and few goods. But neither did they have many worries, and they seldom had to exert themselves.

In addition, Russians today see around them what they call "capitalist" practices (piracy, murder, dishonesty, malevolent and treacherous intentions, blatant disregard of signed contracts, etc.). They see a wild economy unrestrained by law, morality, or internalized moral virtues. Who could love such a moral cesspool? And how could it possibly succeed?

Western economists have simply taken for granted the moral capital of the West. They have accepted it as a free lunch, as if it came without cost, like air and water. In fact, Russia's religious and moral capital was built up by one thousand years of patient development. But under seventy years of communist mockery and abuse, such cultural capital has been covered with filth and sludge. In three generations, Russia's moral tradition has been buried so thoroughly that not more than a tiny flock of living persons has had full access to the moral knowledge possessed by their grandparents. Traditions, like oxygen-bearing lifelines, have been cut.

Virtue, in this sense, is a public as well as a private reality. It is built up, nourished, celebrated, criticized, revised, and in other ways kept vital by entire nations. Virtue has its own proper social ecology. The ethos of each city teaches the young many tacit yet crucial lessons. Praise and blame, celebration and stigma, make especially potent impressions on the young.

As this example from Russia shows, the integrity of business practices depends on the virtue of the people who constitute its many firms. To understand the moral vitality of business in a particular nation, it is necessary to understand not only what moral virtue is but how it is shaped by entire cities. To understand the culture of virtue, we need to understand such key concepts as habit, virtue, character, person, reflection, and choice.

Alas, the word *virtue* today is but a shadow of its former self. Its range of reference is frequently limited to sexual behavior, as when it is said in old books that a woman has lost her "virtue," meaning her chastity. In this weak meaning, the term is practically useless. Yet free societies today—and business, too—cannot function successfully among peoples who lack certain crucial virtues.

Further, the responsibilities imposed on citizens by modern freedoms require a larger spectrum of virtues, and a deeper analysis of virtue, than the ancient Greeks and Romans bequeathed us. Yet because the Greeks were at least clear in their thinking, they take us a long way toward our goal.

VIRTUE IN THE ANCIENT CITY

Athens at the height of its power consisted of 30,000 inhabitants, most of them slaves. To defend their city against their enemies and to attain the sort of civilization to which they aspired, the relatively few free Greek males of Athens had to develop a broad repertoire of military and civil skills.

In their own lives, they needed a certain degree of discipline, self-control, and concentration of attention. For their common life, they needed to learn arts of expression and persuasion, civic duty and public honor, reliability and wisdom. They also needed to learn how to use arms—dagger, sword, spear—and they needed skill with horses and chariots.

A young lad of ten or twelve had quite a lot to learn by the time he reached eighteen. The city needed him to learn these things, and his fellows expected him to learn them. In this context, the word *virtue*—meaning the habits, skills, and dispositions to be learned—corresponded to obvious necessities of Greek cities. (No less do modern cities need specific virtues.)

A Greek male needed to be able to act in many different capacities because the demands of civilization were so many while citizens were few. (On the whole, only males participated in public life.) At one moment, he would need to employ the arts of peace; at another, the arts of war. A sign of a young lad's having mastered the necessary habits was his ability to act quickly, with some degree of excellence and pleasure, in one field of activity and then another.

The most general term for such settled dispositions or capacities is *habit*. From the point of view of either the individual or the community, the Greeks spoke of *good habits* and *bad habits*. The good habits were called "virtues," the bad habits "vices."

The habits were thought of as tendencies or dispositions; in this respect, they were regarded as acquired characteristics of the human mind and will. Such characteristics might be latent since birth, but whether inborn or acquired with great effort, virtues are developed and perfected only through practice. Mind and willpower must be applied through regular exercises.

The word *mind* came into special play when human actions awaited light from insight and judgment. Typical evidences of the human mind in action are paying close attention, sizing up a situation, getting the point of a joke or a story, grasping what needs to be done, forming a judgment that one should proceed in this way rather than in that. All these are acts connected to insight or judgment—and also acts in which experience and observation nourish native wit.

Getting the point about the habits of the mind was, for the Greeks, as natural as opening their eyes. Becoming conscious of the meaning of the word *will* was a little more difficult, as it is also for many people today. Suppose that in going to bed at night you remember that you need to get up the instant the alarm rings, because of an early commitment. However, when the alarm rings, it penetrates your grogginess only gradually. Your sense of hearing and your remote memory awaken first. Later, quite slowly, the mind comes to focus. The action of the will comes last. Here is how it works.

Dimly, you become sufficiently aware of the cause of the jangling to recognize that it comes from an alarm. Slowly, the mind arrives at the need to rise immediately. Instinctively, your arm begins to stir. But neither your mind nor your will is sufficiently focused to direct it efficiently toward the clock.

Your mind becomes dreamily conscious of where you are, what is happening, what that sound means, and what you are expected to do. But your body is still wed to sleep, and the desire for continued union with sleep is strong. The imperative concerning what you ought to do is at war with what your body wants to do. Two parts of yourself are at war: the part attuned to "want" and the part attuned to "ought."

As your mind clarifies, this inner conflict comes into focus. You experience within yourself the slow awakening of will, over against the inclination of the rest of you. Your will is the deepest and last of your inner capacities to come awake. It is the hardest to bring into exercise. You can feel the struggle to summon it up, in order to force yourself to get out of bed.

From this example, it is fairly easy to see why moral education needs to focus on the training of the will. Will is the capacity that tells us to choose to do something or to choose not to. A good will urges us to do what we know we should do, and to want to do so badly enough to overcome the most intense resistance from other parts of our being. (My father used to joke that he had no problems with willpower; what caused him trouble, he said, was *won't* power. What he wanted, he wanted; saying "no" was the harder exercise.) The will is the power to carry the judgment of the mind—"yes" or "no"—into action. It is the power behind self-government, self-mastery, self-discipline.

PASSIONS AND REASON

The example of the alarm clock leads to another point. In Greek thought, particularly in Aristotle, there was considerable clarity about the nature of mind. But of what St. Paul was later to call the "inner war in our members" there was considerably less awareness. The Greeks tended to be fascinated by the power of mind and reason. They didn't give as much scope to will as, later, Christian thought was obliged to, in the light of Christian experience.

Aware of the power of sensuality and pride, the Greeks had an acute sense of the war between reason and the passions. This war reflects in part the famous mind-body problem that still plagues those parts of modern philosophy that owe most to the retrieval of Greek thought by the Enlightenment. (This war between reason and the passions is still vividly at work in the novels of that modern Greek Nikos Kazantzakis, for example, in *The Last Temptation of Christ*.) But this war reflects, as well, and in some ways more profoundly, the hidden work of the passions in subverting, overpowering, or co-opting the mind, of which the Greeks with their love for mind were painfully aware.

The Greeks did not think of passion mainly in terms of sensuality or erotic desire, as moderns often do. The passions of the spirit, the Greeks knew, are deeper and more potent than the passions of the flesh—perhaps especially such passions of the spirit as the desire for power, the pride of life, and the desire for self-sufficiency (the desire to be like God). This fact is still reflected in our own instinctive association of the passions of the spirit with the strong, and the passions of the flesh with the weak. It is a matter of experience that passions of the spirit are more lasting and more deeply driven. Those of the body, while for a time fully and sweetly absorbing, are more quickly sated and in their swift passing leave disquieting emptiness.

The Greeks had a great respect for the passions of the

mind, to which they were deeply committed. So much power did they ascribe to the mind that they sometimes seemed to say that if you knew what you should do, *really knew*, you would necessarily do it. They thought of the Good, fully seen, as overpowering the mind. They did not allow—or did not allow much—for weakness of the will. The action of the will hardly figured in Greek thought.

Thus was left to Christian thinkers, especially to St. Paul, St. Augustine, and St. Thomas Aquinas, the task of explaining how it could happen that what we know we should not do, we do, and what we know we should do, we do not. Regarding the concepts of both conscience and will, Christian philosophy was to add a great deal of light to the unfinished psychology of the Greeks.

Business practices depend critically on a number of effective virtues, and one can understand the virtues only in the context of passions and emotions. In Greek thought, one of the roles of the chief virtues, on which sound human action most hinges (thus the term "cardinal" virtues, from the Latin *cardo*, "hinge"), is *to order the passions in such a way that mind and will can do their best work*. No one can think straight when his or her passions rage. Calm deliberation requires a sort of wall around an inner castle—habits that protect a person's reason from some of the distractions of a disordered life.

Equanimity of mind and will needs at least four things: (1) tempered passions, (2) the courage to quiet fears and inner terrors, (3) practical wisdom, and (4) the right touch in giving to each person and each matter its due. These four habits have been named the "four cardinal virtues": temperance, fortitude, practical wisdom, and justice. We will return to them.

The inner life of the human being, experience taught the Greeks, is complex. One part of ourselves, then another part, seems to take the lead in our consciousness and to display itself in our actions. We act from reason; we act from passion; we act from whim. Thus, the imperative "Know thyself!," a fundamental imperative of human life, gives scope to a wide-ranging inquiry into everything our consciousness touches—including, potentially, the entire universe.

In applying the imperative of self-knowledge to understanding their own human actions, the Greeks laid special stress on those dispositions or capacities from which actions are elicited as situations demand. A man of well-developed habits in a broad range of fields of activity, a well-rounded man, will at one time be called upon to think clearly, on another occasion to speak persuasively, on yet another to lead a group of fellow citizens decisively and wisely, and on a fourth occasion to meet the enemy in deadly and fateful combat.

To perform well in all these fields of activity—and to perform well on demand, with excellence, and with pleasure—is to draw on considerable human capital, derived from inherited and acquired habit. Up until the modern era, the ancient Greeks and Romans, and later the medieval Jews and Christians, attached high importance to education in the virtues most needed by the city.

REFLECTION AND CHOICE

> It has been frequently remarked that it seems to have been reserved to the people of this country, by their conduct and example, to decide the important question, whether societies of men are really capable or not of establishing good government from *reflection* and *choice*, or whether they are forever destined to depend for their political constitutions on accident and force.
>
> —*Alexander Hamilton*

What is it that is most distinctive of human beings? What most makes us human? The answer is two sets of abilities: the mind to gain insight and to make judgments, and the will to lock onto goals and commitments. Each of us deploys these abilities with a distinctive signature that limns our character, as others see us.

These two capacities, to reflect and to choose, give rise to a distinctive language about humans. We are not only "individuals" (as cats are) but "persons" (as cats are not). Our dignity as persons derives from our capacities to reflect and to choose, that is, our capacity to be self-determining and responsible for our own destiny. When people speak of human dignity, they are pointing to this responsibility for self-governance.

Entrepreneurs looking for good help are going to seek out persons capable of taking responsibility many times a day. They need people who pay attention, think critically, discern reality dispassionately, and know how to make decisions. Self-starters can reflect and make decisions—good ones—on their own.

In this light, to take possession of one's own capacity for personhood in everyday life is to train oneself in the full range of habits that allow one to make as many free acts of reflection and choice as possible. A human being at birth is not yet a realized person but does have the potential to become one. That will mean learning a multitude of good habits, including those that allow one to increase the frequency of one's acts of reflection and choice.

Note the paradox here. Each of us must learn many habits in order to be able to bring reflection and choice into play frequently, that is, to act from more than mere habit: to act from choice.

It is not as easy to act from reflection and choice as you might at first think. If you are capable of self-criticism, you will discern soon enough that a great many of the actions you have already taken today were performed mostly by routine, out of habit, without much reflection and choice. And even where "choice" may have been thought to enter, as when at breakfast you poured a glass of orange juice rather than apple juice, an outsider may doubt whether this was more than a learned preference, more than mere taste or inclination. Such "choices," a skeptical observer might say, are not matters much thought about and consciously chosen, not, at least, with that degree of determination and commitment we intend by the word *will*.

Indeed, throughout each long day, we surprisingly seldom exercise our capacities for fresh reflection and conscious choice. Perhaps it is just as well. Perhaps that would be far too tiring. Whatever the reason, we do not often act at the top of our spiritual nature, in the realm of insight and will.

We typically live in their derived light, a kind of moonlight cast from a distance. A lot of our living is spent in a kind of sleepwalking.

All of us, for modern purposes, need fairly clear notions of "habit," "virtue," "mind," "will," and "person"—these terms that are as crucial for a democratic republic as for business. Political leaders, athletes, journalists, doctors, and other professionals need the virtues that the Greeks, Romans, and medieval Jews and Christians knew are important to a good life. Business life now could not be conducted without them.

PRACTICAL WISDOM AND OTHER VIRTUES

Aristotle identified "practical wisdom" (*phronesis*) as the capacity to order all the parts of the self and all the components of action in a realistic and effective way. The person of practical wisdom is like an archer, Aristotle said. In action, there are an infinite number of ways to get things wrong; but to act in the right way, at the right time, with the right emphasis, with regard to the right persons, and with exact appreciation for all the relevant circumstances, is to "hit the mark exactly," like an arrow thudding into a bull's-eye. A good archer has to account not only for the wind but for the weight of his own arrowhead, the defects of his own shaft, the perfection of the feathering, the tensile strength of his bow, the quality of his string, the tightness in his arm, the habits of his own eye, and a whole host of other factors grasped better by instinct and habit than by conscious articulation.

Furthermore, practical wisdom must suffuse all the other virtues, if they are to be on target. Given the Greek love for form, for the shaping loveliness of things, it was natural for them to speak of practical wisdom as the form of all the other virtues. Practical wisdom directs and gives shape to every other virtue while organizing them together in as beautiful a way as possible.

Indeed, the Greeks spoke of goodness under a word, *kalos*, that works as well for beauty as for loveliness. *Kalos* signifies a kind of grace in action. Goodness is to get everything right, to pay the proper reverence to every aspect of things. A good action hits the mark in all respects. When an action is in some way deficient, from one point of view or another, its goodness is marred. Sound business practices depend heavily on *kalos*.

Sadly, the role of *kalos* in moral life has been lost in the modern tradition, with its emphasis on duty. The modern tradition after Kant speaks of morals largely in terms of "duty," "ought," "thou shalt" and "thou shalt not." In sharp contrast, when Aristotle needed a metaphor for goodness in action, he turned to athletics rather than to law or command or duty, as in his example of the archer's "hitting the mark." To him, a good action represented not so much a law obeyed as an instance of beauty in act.

The Greeks sought the Good as an elusive ideal, a goal up ahead to aspire to, a power of attraction and beauty drawing each of us onward by its radiance. The Greeks felt drawn by something, attracted by something, pulled toward it as by some law of the spirit parallel to the physical law of gravity. They called this force that attracted them from the future, up ahead, the Final End. (Another word for this Final End is Omega—as in Alpha [beginning] and Omega.) They thought of ethics, in this sense, as teleology, the pursuit of this attractive and compelling End. They conceived of this End as a transformation in ourselves, but most of all not extrinsic to us but, rather, fully immanent, intrinsic, and transformative.

To reflect on ethics, in Aristotle's view, is to try to imagine what sort of person one wishes to be by the end of one's life. The idea is that we must discover ourselves—learn who we are, who we were made to be—and, in another sense, we must *make* ourselves, shape ourselves according to the model of the ideal man or woman, as best we can discern that ideal.

The most workable path here is to choose a living model, as Aristotle chose Pericles, and to learn to make choices in the way Pericles would make them. This, Aristotle says, is the path to practical wisdom: to single out an exemplar in advance and then begin working to develop the habits required to live like that exemplar. Of course, we should not copy him, only study how he reached decisions, acted, made corrections in his life voyage. Among these habits, the Greeks thought (as we have seen), we would need not only practical wisdom but also justice, temperance, and courage.

To the four cardinal virtues (practical wisdom, justice, temperance, and courage) the Western tradition down the years has added a host of others: magnanimity, liberality, patience, perseverance, sympathy, fellow-feeling, benevolence, and the like, not to mention such distinctively Christian virtues, at a later period, as faith, hope, charity, humility, kindness, and (in this context only one among many, but a jewel) chastity.

The list of virtues beloved by the premoderns eventually became quite long, for one had only to observe or to feel the need for new human excellences to add new virtues to the list. In our own age of democratic politics and new social conditions, we have need of many new virtues. We won't spend further time on developing a list here, but in chapter 6 will consider three virtues essential to modern business life.

Some virtues are obviously in conflict with one another; when is patience cowardice, or temperance pettiness? Few persons, and probably none, are endowed by nature with all the virtues or have time to master all of them equally. In practice, different persons choose different favorites. Every person develops a fairly unique blend of habits. We call this unique package of habits, good and bad, *character*.

To have character is to have a fairly defined profile of habits that can be relied upon, that have, as it were, a kind of personal stamp: "That sounds just like him." "That is completely out of character for her; I never saw her do anything like that."

From *virtue*, therefore, we arrive at *character*. Character is a personal quiverful of virtues (and vices), a distinctive repertoire of more or less predictable dispositions.

There we have it. A rather rough and ready definition of terms. Henceforth, at least, when we speak of "habit" and "virtue," "character" and "act," "reflection" and "choice," "mind" and "will," and "passions of the spirit" and "passions of the flesh," we should have a fairly clear idea of what we mean.

A MODERN CULTURE OF VIRTUE?

Ethics, Aristotle wrote, is a branch of politics. Long before we are able to choose for ourselves, throughout our childhood and even adolescence, our city—our *polis* or political regime—shapes us more than we shape ourselves. But this is not the whole story.

We dare not ignore those alternating acts of rebellion and self-appropriation, dissent and enthusiastic approbation, that each person makes as he or she goes along, nodding or frowning at, imitating or rejecting, the panoramic scene and passing parade.

However strong their conditioning, persons do in the end define themselves. That is why people are so endlessly fascinating in their inexhaustible variety.

Nonetheless, city differs from city, and constitution from constitution. The shape of the institutions they live under goes a long way toward determining the kinds of character its citizens are likely to develop. Thus, many persons today do not like the modern city they are living in.

Still, when such persons demand a return to the ancient moral virtues, they sometimes falsify the past. In reaction against the politicization of modern life, they seek refuge in the quieter gardens in which the practice of the personal virtues is assiduously cultivated, as in a cloister.

They forget that Aristotle was not writing about life in the cloister but life in the city. They forget the public nature, and the public role, of the virtues he was describing. Such public virtues were absolutely necessary to the survival and the flourishing of Athens. Insofar as Athens was one high point of civilization, its achievement depended on the Athenian virtues. Those were the chief form of human capital in Athens. These virtues were not merely private; their role was public and visible. Perish those virtues, perish Athens.

So it is with any nation today. To be sure, societies constructed around sets of institutions different from those of Athens call forth a different panoply of virtues. But crucial virtues they do require. As James Madison once said, it is chimerical to think that a republic (such as he wished the United States to be) can thrive without the practice of republican virtues.

Above all, then, virtue is learned in social contexts. We learn from others how to improve our moral skills. We are encouraged—or ridiculed—by others. If in society as a whole we wish again to regard every criminal as "an enemy of the human race," as the criminal was regarded in the America of Tocqueville's time, we also need to praise every man and woman of virtue as our friend.

Four obstacles stand in the way.

✧ First, our high culture—composed of intellectuals, professors, and artists—is quite ambivalent about praise
for virtue and for character, as it is also ambivalent
about strengthening the family. For many, such realities
smack of "traditional values"—those residues of the
dark past that "enlightenment" is supposed to
"enlighten" us from.

✧ Second, our academic tradition in the study of ethics
has largely ignored the concepts of virtue and character.
(This neglect is not unrelated to its neglect of the moral
worth of business as a calling.) While the Aristotelian
tradition is kept alive in Great Britain and (outside the
Catholic intellectual tradition) rather less so in the
United States, it seldom counts for a great deal in contemporary ethical discussion, and its concepts are
almost never clearly grasped or accurately presented.

Thus, if one were to ask contemporary intellectuals to
define "virtue" and "character," there is reason to doubt, first,
whether discussions of significant clarity would be forthcoming;
and, second, whether the powerful arguments of the past would
be known well enough to be embodied within them. Instead,
amid disparaging allusions to the "Victorian age" and "bourgeois morality," progressives are likely to suggest that virtue and
character connote a straitlaced, stiff, hypocritical, and conservative moral posture, from which they intend to "liberate" us.

These are serious intellectual errors of distortion and omis-
sion with serious consequences. If clear concepts of virtue and
character are not available at the highest intellectual level, it is
not likely that they will be taken seriously in textbooks, curric-
ula, and informed public discussion.

✧ Third, today's entertainment media to some extent dis-
parage virtue and character and to some extent totally

depend on them. The essential dependence of the media on virtue and character follows from the inherent demands of the art of storytelling. Without character, "characters" would lack intelligibility; without virtue, they could not be attractive. Courage, kindness, tenderness, persistence, integrity, loyalty, and other virtues are indispensable to the storyteller's art.

On the other hand, audiences love plots in which heroes and heroines are tempted, fall, flout conventions, "kick against the goad," and in other ways rebel—at least against excessively conventional ways of understanding virtue and character. In a profound sense, such real-life battles deepen our understanding of true virtue, true character, and "true grit."

In a superficial sense, however, popular entertainment often depends on shock value and titillation. Its producers are always tempted to violate ethical norms just enough to offer a taste of forbidden fruit, yet without creating too high a sense of alarm. When this is done in cheap and tawdry fashion—through unnecessary nudity, violent behavior, and mere impulse gratification—critics properly attack such products on aesthetic and moral grounds. Yet producers of television shows and popular films often want it both ways: they both pander to public vices and resent being attacked as foes of traditional values. (For further comments on this point, see chapter 7.)

> Fourth, there is in the mass media a striking absence of significant drama about the specific struggles for virtue and character characteristic of the Jewish and Christian traditions. Ordinarily, persons do not learn "virtue in general"; rather, through their families and religious traditions, they learn particular paths to virtue, taught somewhat distinctively within each religious body.

Some religious bodies are quite impulsive, for example, placing great stress on vivid emotional experiences in moments of conversion ("I accepted Jesus the day after my birthday, in 1972," one such communicant may recall). Others have more sober, restrained traditions that appeal much less to subjective experience and far more to objective disciplines and rites. Virtue, in the concrete, is typically communicated through particular communities of understanding, method, and style.

In short, for many reasons and from many directions, unusual obstacles have been thrown up in our culture to the development of a healthy public ethos. Elites worry openly about the ecology of our physical environment but far too little about our moral ecology. These obstacles to an ethos of virtue do not inhere in capitalism; on the contrary, they are destructive of capitalism. One hesitates to invite businesspeople to become censors of what goes on in the media they own or in the shows for which they are the advertising sponsors. But they really must reexamine their responsibilities in this regard, much more critically than they have been doing.

In matters affecting the ecology of liberty—affecting the habits of a reflective and deliberate, self-governing citizenry—laissez-faire is not good enough. Owners and advertisers must also be responsible, and with calm and long-range deliberation decide which messages they will *not* promulgate because they are destructive of the habits of liberty. To undermine the virtues of our families and our citizens is social suicide.

People in business have got to be serious about their public moral responsibilities, especially their responsibilities for the messages that dominate our public airwaves, movies, and music.

Ironically, business can become the chief counterweight to the moral decadence now evident on the airwaves simply by *connecting with the concerns of ordinary citizens*. We all have a vested interest—national survival—in the state of the public ethos.

OUR INCURIOUS ELITES

Our intellectual and academic elites have been remarkably incurious about virtue and religion for some years, and our national communications media have been (at least until recent years) remarkably reticent about them. Most seem eager to explore "new" moralities, fresh "liberations," new imperatives of "consciousness raising," and the ongoing saga of "progressive" attitudes. The bias is pronounced. It exacts several social costs.

One such cost appears to be a gap between the cultures of academic and intellectual elites and those of the ordinary public. Another seems to be the vacuum created by the growing separation of the three major subsystems of our political economy: political, economic, and moral-cultural. This point needs some explication.

While emphasizing the republic's dependence on the virtue and religiousness of its citizens, the American founders did not assign to government (except in designing the *Polis*) the daily task of "soulcraft." This they left to the leaders of the nation's moral and cultural institutions: principally to families, of course, and local communities, but also to the churches, the press (today, the "media"), and the universities and schools.

For generations, the primary task explicitly assigned to the public schools (which did not appear until the 1840s) was character formation. Filled with biblical sayings and religious sentiments, *McGuffey's Reader* exemplified the methods employed in teaching reading, writing, and arithmetic. America's children learned from them not only techniques but classic statements of American purpose and American (Protestant) virtue.

In recent decades, by contrast, the teaching of virtue and character has explicitly *not* been the primary function of the American state-run public schools. Virtue has been replaced by moral neutrality.

Further, the American mainline churches no longer seem to emphasize their long traditions of instruction in virtue and character but, rather, to emphasize counseling, therapeutic methods, and social causes. In the university world, too, emphasis on virtue and character would now seem to many not only quaint but threatening and impermissible.

Thus, no major institution today appears to concern itself with the standing of virtue and character in modern culture. Virtue and character have been orphaned.

The results have been predictable—and dreary. By a kind of happy error, William Bennett noted in his *Index of Leading Cultural Indicators* that the most serious problems teachers identified in the nation's public schools in 1940 were (ranked in this order): talking out of turn; chewing gum; making noise; running in the halls; cutting in line; dress code violations; and littering. Taken in 1990, a later survey discovered a far different ranking of problems in the schools: drug abuse; alcohol abuse; pregnancy; suicide; rape; robbery; and assault. It turns out that no one can find those surveys. (Bennett's source misled him, and he has withdrawn the point in later editions.) Still, for those who lived through both periods, these new worries (which are real enough) are not indicators of progress.

Understandably, then, families concerned to instruct their children in virtue and character feel isolated and alone. From the glowing screen in their own living rooms, and not infrequently even by permissive cultural elites on all sides, their dearest values are publicly undermined.

Employers are finding fewer workers who have been taught sufficient discipline to learn even basic reading, writing, and arithmetic, let alone such fundamental work habits as showing up every day, on time, ready to work, and able to practice basic courtesies in dealing with others.

This highly visible decline in virtue does not entail that the future is inexorably bleak. On the contrary, many families and local communities have shown themselves to be amazingly resilient and persistent in continuing to instruct their youngsters in the classic paths of virtue and of character. In some ways, such institutions of immediate culture may prove to be more powerful than the remote cultures represented through nationwide institutions.

There are significant indications, furthermore, that a quiet moral revolution is underway, affecting not only communications elites but, in particular, some of the more influential intellectual and academic elites. In America, even "progressive" elites are thinking and writing these days—at last!—about the family, local communities, civil society, and traditional values. William Bennett's skillful anthology, *The Book of Virtues*, has wrung warm praise from left and right alike.

Even "progressives," they are now insisting, depend on moral appeals to commitment, integrity, sacrifice for a cause, comradely bonds, honesty, and individual initiative. Many former socialists are expressing new-found pleasure in having practiced the old, prosaic working-class virtues for decades now—loyalty, honesty, fidelity to spouse and family, patriotism, self-sacrifice, and thrift—even though they had forgotten for two or three decades how to speak of them. On the virtues, Tony Blair, the new leader of Britain's Labour party, often sounds like former prime minister Thatcher.

BUSINESS DEPENDS ON VIRTUE

Business has a vested interest in virtue. It cannot go forward with realism, courage, wisdom, honesty, and integrity without a highly motivated and virtuous work community. It cannot endure without leaders and colleagues in whom many key virtues are internalized. In this and in many other ways, business is dependent on the moral and cultural institutions of the free society: families especially, schools, and public civic life. A nation's moral culture is even more fundamental than its physical ecology.

Moreover, there is a reason that traditional morality is called "bourgeois morality." The practice of business sets high moral requirements, which depend for their fulfillment on the

human capital of both classical and modern virtues living in the
people. As one Nobel Prize economist has asked, "Just how
much is the Japanese work ethic worth to the economy of
Japan?" An incalculable amount.

In free societies, in brief, the language of virtue and character is indispensable—so indispensable as to be prosaic. How
can a people profess to be capable of self-government in public life if they cannot govern their passions in private life? How
can a people govern a whole society that cannot, each of them,
govern themselves? In the free society, virtue is a sine qua non.
Where there is no virtue, the free society perishes, and the very
idea of liberty becomes chimerical.

The "new science of politics" that led to the American
founding drank deeply of the wisdom of the Greeks and
Romans. You can see this on every page of *The Federalist*—just
as you can see classic virtues on every page of Shakespeare.
The Bible, Socrates, Aristotle, Cicero, Seneca, Shakespeare:
these were the moral teachers of our forebears.

Yet the American founders also recognized that the republic they reared here had "no model on the face of the globe,"
and they feared not to speak of *novus ordo seclorum*—"a new
order for the ages." They recognized that to the list of the classical virtues, new virtues suited to a new republic needed to be
discerned and cultivated.

Our task now is to single out some of those new virtues
(not unrelated to the classical virtues)—at least three of
them—that are of particular significance to business. These are
the virtues that, in the practicing thereof, yield delight in excellence and mastery.

Happiness is not a feeling. Nor is it a sentiment. It is a practice—the practice of excellence in action. The really good people in business (as in other challenging fields) taste it often.

Chapter Six

✙

THREE CARDINAL VIRTUES OF BUSINESS

Indeed, besides the earth, man's principal resource is *man himself*. His intelligence enables him to discover the earth's productive potential and the many different ways in which human needs can be satisfied. It is his disciplined work in close collaboration with others that makes possible the creation of ever more extensive *working communities* which can be relied upon to transform man's natural and human environments. Important virtues are involved in this process, such as diligence, industriousness, prudence in undertaking reasonable risks, reliability and fidelity in interpersonal relationships, as well as courage in carrying out decisions which are difficult and painful but necessary, both for the overall working of a business and in meeting possible setbacks.

—Pope John Paul II

When a person who has never been in business before decides
to risk his life savings on an idea that he is sure will work, some
of his associates, perhaps his spouse and his brother or sister,
and even an adviser or two, will tell him he is going to lose his
shirt. "If it could be done," one of them will say, "somebody
would have done it." Some persons nevertheless have the self-
confidence and the courage to plough ahead. They think that
others are misdiagnosing reality and overlooking certain factors. In addition, the entrepreneur is pretty sure he can form a
good team of associates and that all of them together can get
the job done. Somehow Pope John Paul II understands this,
and in the first half of this chapter I will often be paraphrasing
points he made in *Centesimus Annus*.

When my friend Phil Merrill decided the time for setting
off on his own was now or never, he was a young and lower-
level government worker, married, with two kids. He thought
he would make a good publisher; he was looking for a newspa-
per or magazine to buy. It had to be cheap, because he didn't
have much money. When an opportunity came up to buy a
small paper in Annapolis, Maryland, he decided to go for it. He
had to mortgage his house to the hilt for the down payment,
and even then needed to borrow from friends who did not have
much to lend. While basically supportive, his wife, Ellie,
remembers being pretty worried about the whole deal. There
would be a lot of problems at the new paper—moving in on an
old family enterprise, dealing with existing staff, and trying to
make changes with no capital to spare. At that time, a lot of
small newspapers were failing, killed off by both television and
large regional papers with special local editions.

Looking at such examples and many others, I have tried to
discern the sorts of habits an entrepreneur needs in order to
succeed. There are many necessary habits, but three seem central. Simply to succeed in business—even if for no higher
motive than success—these three virtues are essential. I call

them cardinal virtues in the same sense that, as we saw in the last chapter, the ancient Greeks and Romans spoke of the four cardinal virtues of a happy human life: they are like hinges on which success—in life and in business—swings.

Success in living a happy life is a larger project than success in business, and nearly everybody in business wants to achieve both. But they are not quite the same thing, and here I concentrate on the three virtues especially central to success in business. (An inquisitive reader could draw out parallels between the two sets of cardinal virtues.)

The three cardinal virtues of business are *creativity, building community*, and *practical realism*. Obviously each of these good habits requires the support of other good habits. Creativity, for example, needs courage, hard work, and persistence. Building community requires honesty, generosity, and a spirit of justice. And realism implies a capacity to listen, pay attention, stay alert, and take a broad view, as well as a capacity for self-criticism and self-correction.

All these are virtues necessary for workers all down the line, not only in the glamorous positions. They satisfy a human need for personal commitment and excellence.

THE VIRTUE OF CREATIVITY

> The ultimate resource in economic development is people. It is people, not capital or raw materials, that develop an economy. The greatest need in the underdeveloped countries is people who can do the new organizing job, the job of building an effective organization of skilled and trained people exercising judgment and making responsible decisions.
>
> —*Peter F. Drucker*

Most of us first learned to think about the ethic of capitalism from Max Weber's *The Protestant Ethic and the Spirit of*

Capitalism (1904). It was Weber's great achievement to bring to consciousness the fact that cultural forces are essential to the definition of capitalism; capitalism is not a system solely about things but about the human spirit. Nonetheless, there is some question whether Max Weber actually caught the spirit of capitalism in his sights. I think he scored a near-miss. He thought the essence of capitalism is calculation, a strictly cost-conscious analysis of means in relation to ends. He saw in it the growth of bureaucracy, like a rushing locomotive that would confine human spontaneity to "iron rails." He seemed to have in mind the huge industrial enterprises of the turn of the century, and he expressed some dread of the advancing locomotive.

In all this, he missed something much closer to the heart of the matter: discovery, invention, serendipity, surprise—what my colleague Rocco Buttiglione of the International Academy of Philosophy in Lichtenstein (and now chairman of Italy's new party, Christian Democrats United) calls the "Don Quixote factor."

At the very heart of capitalism, as Friedrich Hayek, Joseph Schumpeter, and the American Israel Kirzner have shown, is the creative habit of enterprise. Enterprise is, in its first moment, the inclination to notice, the habit of discerning, the tendency to discover what other people don't yet see. It is also the capacity to act on insight, so as to bring into reality things not before seen. It is the ability to foresee both the needs of others and the combinations of productive factors most adapted to satisfying those needs. This habit of intellect constitutes an important source of wealth in modern society. Organizing such a productive effort, planning its duration in time, making sure that it corresponds in a positive way to the demands it must satisfy, and taking the necessary risks: all this has been a source of new wealth in the past 200 years. In this way, the role of initiative and entrepreneurial ability have become increasingly decisive.

Many critics seem never to have imagined the sheer fun and creative pleasure involved in bringing a new business to birth. Such creativity has the stamp of a distinctive personality all over it. In the pleasure it affords its creator, it rivals, in its way, artistic creativity.

To verify this, visit a business in the presence of its builder. It is quite possible that no actress was ever so pleased with her standing-ovation performance as an entrepreneur is with what she has built. Note, too, that a rapidly increasing proportion of entrepreneurs worldwide is female; enterprise is a vocation made to order for newcomers into markets.

In precapitalist centuries, the chief form of wealth was land. For thousands of years, the natural fruitfulness of the earth was the primary factor of wealth; work and invention were bent to the increase of this fruitfulness. Under capitalism, the newcomer among economic systems, enterprise turned work in new directions. Enterprise itself—invention and discovery and new ideas—became the most dynamic source of wealth the world had ever known.

In brief, the new system linked work more and more with knowledge. *And this is the crucial switch*. This is the point missed by some (like Marx) who hold to the labor theory of value. It is not so much labor, in the sense of physical labor, that adds value, but working *smart*—adding enterprise and invention to everything one does. Work becomes ever more fruitful and productive to the extent that people become more knowledgeable of the productive potentialities of the earth and more profoundly cognizant of the needs of those for whom their work is done. The cause of wealth is knowledge. This cause lies in the human mind.

"What is the cause of the wealth of nations?" This is the question that Adam Smith was the first to raise in 1776; Pope Leo XIII alluded to it in *Rerum Novarum* in 1891. Pope John Paul II, a hundred years later, had his own crisp reply:

In our time, in particular, there exists another form of ownership which is becoming no less important than land: *the possession of know-how, technology and skill*. The wealth of the industrialized nations is based much more on this kind of ownership than on natural resources.

The chief cause of wealth is intellectual capital. Since the wealth of nations is based much more on intellectual property and know-how than on natural resources, some nations that are very wealthy in natural resources (such as Brazil) may remain poor, while other nations that have virtually no natural resources (like Japan) can become among the richest in the world.

Whereas at one time the decisive factor of production was the land and later capital—understood (in Marx's sense) as ownership of the means of production—today the decisive factor is increasingly human knowledge, especially scientific knowledge. Yet enterprise depends also on a capacity for interrelated and compact organization, and on an ability to perceive the needs of others and to satisfy them. These are exactly the factors in which Japan is preeminent: scientific knowledge, a capacity for organization, and ability to perceive the needs of others and to satisfy them. Through these factors, the Japanese, whose country is extremely poor in natural resources, have made themselves economically preeminent among the nations.

Of course, natural resources are still important. But if human beings do not see their value and figure out ways to bring them into universal use, natural resources may lie fallow, forever undiscovered and unused. Oil lay beneath the sands of Arabia for thousands of years, unused, regarded as a nuisance, until human beings developed the piston engine and learned how to convert crude oil into gasoline. It is human beings who made useless crude into a "natural resource."

For this reason, inanimate things are not the deepest, best, or most inexhaustible resources. The human mind is, as Julian

Simon puts it, the "ultimate resource." It is not the things of earth that set limits to the wealth of the world. On this question over twenty years ago the Club of Rome, drastically exaggerating the scarcity of material resources, made an elementary mistake. Many of the things of this earth are useful at some times and not at other times—whale oil is a good example—depending on the value the human mind sees in them. In this sense, the mind of human beings is the primary source of wealth. And no wonder: it participates from afar in the source of all knowledge, the Creator. Sharing in God's creativity, so to speak, the principal resource of humans is their own inventiveness. Their intelligence enables them to discover the earth's productive potential, but also the many different ways in which human needs can be satisfied.

Pope John Paul II sees three ways in which human knowledge is a source of wealth. First is the *ability to foresee* both the needs of others and the combinations of productive factors most adapted to satisfying those needs. Second, many goods cannot be adequately produced through the work of an isolated individual; they require the cooperation of many people working toward a common goal. Thus, a second kind of knowledge entails *knowing how to organize the large-scale community* necessary to produce even so simple an object as a pencil.

It does not ordinarily occur to theologians, but it is a matter of everyday experience to businesspeople, that even so simple an object as a pencil is made up of elements of graphite, wood, metal, rubber, and lacquer (to mention only the most visible, and to leave aside others that only specialists know about), which come from vastly separated parts of this earth. The knowledge and skills needed to prepare each one of these separate elements for the precise role they will play in the pencil represent a huge body of scientific and practical knowledge, which is almost certainly not present in the mind of any one individual. On the contrary, it is widely dispersed among researchers, managers, and workers in factories and workplaces in different parts of the world. All of these factors of production—materials, knowledge, and skilled workers—must be brought together before anyone holds a pencil.

So far, we have seen two kinds of knowledge at work in human economic creativity: accurate insight into the needs of others and practical knowledge concerning how to organize a worldwide productive effort. But there is also a third kind: the *painstaking effort to discover the earth's productive potential.* Consider briefly several discoveries whose diffusion has done so much to change the world since 1980: the invention of fiber optics, which in so many places are replacing copper (and thus contributing to the difficulties of Chile's copper industry); the invention of the word processor and electronic processes in general (which are doing so much to shift the basis of industry from mechanical to electronic technologies); the use of satellites and electronic impulses to link the entire world in a single, instantaneous communications network; and many medical breakthroughs, including genetic medicine. Such breathtaking discoveries are the fruit of the principal human resource: creative intelligence.

It is no accident that a capitalist economy grew up first in the part of the world deeply influenced by Judaism and Christianity. Millions of people over many centuries learned from Judaism and Christianity not to regard the earth as a realm merely to accept, never to investigate or experiment with; but, rather, as a place in which to exercise human powers of inquiry, creativity, and invention.

The philosopher Alfred North Whitehead once remarked that the rise of modern science was inconceivable apart from the habits human beings learned during long centuries of tutelage under Judaism and Christianity. Judaism and Christianity taught humans that the whole world and everything in it are intelligible, because all things—even contingent and seemingly accidental events—spring from the mind of an all-knowing Creator. This teaching had great consequences in the practical order.

Man the discoverer is made in the image of God. To be creative, to cooperate in bringing creation itself to its perfection is an important element of the human vocation. This belief that each human being is *imago Dei*—made in the image of God— was bound to lead, in an evolutionary and experimental way, to the development of an economic system whose first premise is that the principal cause of wealth is human creativity.

THE VIRTUE OF BUILDING COMMUNITY

It is becoming clearer every day that one person's work is naturally interrelated with the work of others. More than ever, work is *work with others* and *work for others*. Nearly all work is a matter of doing something for someone else. The community involved in even the humblest work is often the whole world, as Phyllis Jordan of PJ's Coffee reminded us in chapter 1.

From its very beginnings, the modern business economy was designed to become an international system, concerned with raising the "wealth of nations," *all* nations, in a systematic, social way. It was by no means focused solely on the wealth of particular individuals.

As the system touches more and more peoples of the world, the distinctive modern fact is that people work with each other, sharing in a community of work that embraces ever-widening circles. Pencils and autos and thousands of other goods are produced from elements widely scattered around the globe. Indeed, most goods today cannot be produced through the work of an isolated individual. Virtually all require the cooperation of many people working toward a common goal, even while few of them see the whole picture, only their own small corner of it.

Today it takes disciplined work in close collaboration with

others to make possible the creation of ever more extensive working communities, which transform natural and human environments.

In a word, businesspeople are constantly, on all sides, involved in building community. Immediately at hand, in their own firm, they must build a community of work. A great deal depends on the level of creativity, teamwork, and high morale a firm's leaders can inspire.

Next, for its practical operations the firm depends on a larger community of suppliers and customers, bankers and government officials, transport systems and the rule of law.

In the third place—as we saw in the example of the pencil—modern products are constituted by components from every part of the planet. The modern business system expresses the interdependence of the whole human race.

In all three ways, business is a community activity. Capitalism is not solely about the individual. It is about a creative form of community.

Indeed, in its internal composition, the business firm is primarily a community of persons who in various ways are trying to satisfy their basic needs and to form such businesses at the service of the whole society.

Since the business organization must be understood primarily as a community, moreover, profitability is not the only indicator of its condition. It is possible for the financial accounts to be in order and yet for the people who make up the firm's most valuable asset to be oppressed and their dignity grievously offended. This is morally inadmissible. And since such outcomes would eventually have negative repercussions on the firm's economic efficiency, most firms spend considerable energy trying to make the work environment as pleasant as they can, consistent with the discipline imposed by their essential tasks.

In brief, the institution that is capitalism's main contribution to the human race is not individualism; it is the private business corporation, independent of the state. The main thing to notice about this invention is that it generates a new and important form of human community—one of whose main social purposes is to create new wealth beyond the wealth that existed before it came into being. Even the pope notes with approval this aspect of profit: "When a firm makes a profit, this means that productive factors have been properly employed and corresponding human needs have been duly satisfied."

When, through the exercise of knowledge, the business firm uses the productive factors of the earth properly and discerns and satisfies human needs, it is at the service of the whole of society. The economic and the ethical point of a business corporation is to serve others. In its own down-to-earth way, the business firm represents a partial but important form of human community.

In fact, Pope John Paul II went to daring lengths in asserting that the modern business process "throws practical light on a truth about the person which Christianity has constantly affirmed." That truth is this: *the Creator made the human person to work in community and to cooperate freely with other persons, for the sake of other persons.*

This creative community is the greatest transformative power of the condition of the poor on earth. From the bottom up, the business system seeks out persons of talent, initiative, and enterprise who want to better their condition and that of their localities.

The modern business process also instills—and requires—the practice of a number of other virtues, among them diligence, industriousness, prudence in undertaking reasonable risks, reliability, and fidelity in interpersonal relationships. Especially in its leaders, business also requires courage in carrying out decisions that are difficult and painful, but necessary in meeting setbacks.

These ordinary, kitchen-variety virtues should be seen in the context of the basic goodness of creation as it springs from the hands of the Creator. These virtues are not negative, repressive, or ascetic—or at least not primarily so—for they entail invention, serendipity, surprise, and the sort of romance that leads many to risk their shirts. And they are virtues necessary to sustain new forms of community, even an international community embracing all the peoples of the earth.

THE VIRTUE OF PRACTICAL REALISM

The third cardinal virtue of business is related to the classical cardinal virtue of practical wisdom.

I never met a businessman who did not pride himself on being realistic. Even the romantic ones among them (entrepreneurs tend to have broad romantic streaks) are willing to bet their fortunes on being in closer touch with reality than others.

Many of the most innovative have worked their way up from the skunk works and the back rooms, where they have paid their dues by getting their hands dirty and facing day-to-day frustrations. In fact, it is often their strong sense of how the world really works, from the bottom up, that gives them confidence that their new ideas—no matter how unrealistic others may think them—are in touch with reality, and that it is others who are living by illusions.

In academic circles today, realism is regarded as outmoded. There is only opinion: yours, mine, and those of billions of others. There are only "perceptions." Who knows whose perceptions are "true"?

People in business cannot afford to think like that. They are betting their careers (and, sometimes, life savings) on being in touch with reality. It is not that they think that getting things right is easy. They pride themselves on their common sense. They know a lot about chance, luck, contingency, and serendipity. They are happy to seize insights wherever they find them. They are always paying attention, looking out for surprises. A failure to be in touch with reality can bring them to ruin.

Whereas philosophers can afford to hold that we are never in touch with reality but only with "perceptions," people in business have bitter experiences to teach them the palpable difference between perceptions and reality.

A story illustrating that difference appeared in the magazine of the Naval Institute and was given wide circulation by Stephen R. Covey, whose book *The Seven Habits of Highly Effective People* in effect examines seven virtues of the modern city.

One night in a heavy fog, as the commander of a naval vessel is peering left and right with his glasses trying to penetrate the gloom, his attention is called to a light dead ahead.

"Course?" he barks.

"Steady coming on."

The commander ordered a signal flashed to the oncoming ship to change course by 20 degrees.

The other party soon flashed back: "Advisable you change course immediately by 20 degrees."

Angry now, the commander ordered another flash. "I am an admiral and this is a battleship. Immediately change course."

Back flashed the reply: "This is Seaman Second Class Jones, and I'm on a lighthouse. Advisable to change course."

The battleship changed course.

Both parties in this encounter had perceptions. But reality and common sense broke through subjective illusions, through rank and power and appearance, and made a rocklike point about reality. A lighthouse is a lighthouse. In business, it is necessary to keep adjusting perceptions to the contours of reality—and to be on the lookout for mistaken impressions—all the time.

"Five brains are better than one," Paul Oreffice, retired chairman of Dow, likes to recall. "Brainstorming with different guys brings into play different experiences. Warning signs show up. If they don't and you hit a rock, you better get different guys." Executive officers are paid for getting reality right and getting things done.

This doesn't mean that people in business have a wide-angle lens, letting them see everything they need to see. They will be the first to tell you how often things go wrong. They have got to keep their eyes open. "There are a million ways to screw up," Oreffice will tell you. "And we can't afford any of them."

On the debit side, the virtue of realism in business is more narrow-gauged than the classical virtue of practical wisdom. The object on which the classical virtue focuses is the whole reality of a person's life. Its radical questions are: "What sort of person do I wish to become by the time I die? How ought I to live? What steps should I take today?" A person in business may be practicing that classical virtue when thinking about her calling: "How will this calling help me to become the kind of person I want to become?"

Most of the time, though, in the economic part of his life, sticking to his professional list, a businessman's focus is on the good of the firm. What are our priorities? What should we do today? Who's watching out for problem A? Who's covering B? How will we surprise the competition next year?

Business is oriented to action. (Even patents are not given for ideas alone but for "ideas reduced to practice.") Action requires goals. Getting to goals requires strategies. Strategies require tactics. Each must suit the available personnel and other resources. The need for practical realism at every step is obvious.

Acquiring the many habits of mind and will necessary to accomplish such tasks, long range and short range, takes a singleminded concentration of talent, energy, and application. It tests a person.

At the end of the day, there is always the lighthouse test.

Did we escape the rocks? Did we bring the ship into port safely, mission accomplished?

Because life is full of contingencies and surprises, good luck and bad luck, and hazards of timing, professionals who must deal with multiple contingencies every day, and for whom even one big mistake can destroy an entire career, tend to have profound respect for little things. "The devil is in the details." Watchfulness is their daily attitude; it has to be.

Because their state of life is subject to great hazards, professional warriors, athletes, and entrepreneurs have a lot in common. They tend to be unusually aware of how many facets of reality are not under their control, how dependent they are on such factors, and the great difference between being smiled on—or frowned on—by Providence.

One of the inscriptions on the seal of the United States is *Annuit coeptis* ("He smiles on our undertakings"). The author of *The Federalist* No. 37 saw this hand of Providence at work often in our history, especially in its vulnerable condition during the Revolution:

> The real wonder is that so many difficulties should have been surmounted, and surmounted with a unanimity almost as unprecedented as it must have been unexpected. It is impossible for any man of candor to reflect on this circumstance without partaking of the astonishment. It is impossible for the man of pious reflection not to perceive in it a finger of that Almighty hand which has been so frequently and signally extended to our relief in the critical stages of the revolution.

It should not be surprising that in this commercial republic, prayers for the protection of Divine Providence (and of thanksgiving) have always seemed realistic and fitting.

Those whose efforts to better the human community mark them as creators, made in the image of their Creator, develop a mental habit in which prayer seems to accord with the nat-

ural law itself—and even with the law of grace. Many lands
have a patriotic hymn that captures this feeling. Here is our
own version:

> *America! America!*
> *God shed His grace on thee!*

It should hardly be surprising, then, that many persons in
business will tell you that they feel extraordinarily blessed.
Even unbidden, they will tell you how much they owe to this
nation's system, to their colleagues, to their firm—and to
Providence itself. Most of their blessings came from sources
beyond their own efforts. They did their part. They gave their
talents, used them to the full. But their fundamental attitude is
that they have been given far more than they put in.

For this, they are grateful. "Acknowledging and adoring an
overruling Providence," the phrase that Thomas Jefferson used
in his First Inaugural, seems entirely within the bounds of the
realism they admire.

AND DON'T FORGET THE FUN OF IT!

In Pope John Paul II business leaders have at last found an
ecclesiastical leader who sees clearly what moves them, speaks
of that spirit affirmatively, and sets great challenges in front of
them. His encyclical *Centesimus Annus* or *The Hundredth Year*
(1991) sets out a huge agenda. It offers no grounds for com-
placency. It does what no other religious document has done
before: grasps the interiority of the life of business, the excitement of it, the idealism of it, the challenge of it. Men and
women of business *enjoy* creating something that did not exist
before.

Further, there is nothing business leaders like better than
challenges. So it would be surprising if men and women of

business are not stimulated by the pope's words to become more creative than ever and to lead the way to the revolution in the world's economy that the pope envisages.

Business ethics means a great deal more than obeying the civil law and not violating the moral law. It means imagining and creating a new sort of world based on the principles of individual creativity, community, realism, and the other virtues of enterprise. It means respecting the right of the poor to their own personal economic initiative and their own creativity. It means fashioning a culture worthy of free women and free men—to the benefit of the poor and to the greater glory of God.

In this light, business ethics means meeting the responsibilities of corporations and small businesses. Some of these responsibilities may not seem like "ethics" at all. They are simply the behaviors necessary to make a business succeed. But that's the point. Quite *internal* to business are significant moral hurdles that need to be jumped—before you even come to the ethical requirements imposed on business from outside in, by the standards of religious convictions, moral principles, an adequate humanism, and human rights.

Often business ethicists do not notice these internal moral imperatives. But if they would inspect cultures in which these internal responsibilities are not respected (such as Russia in the 1990s)—in which the murderous law of the jungle prevails—they might see that internalized virtues and practices, even if silent and kept tacit, are crucially important.

Using the number seven biblically—to signify an unlimited number—we turn now to "seven plus seven" business responsibilities. Such weighty responsibilities demand participants who have mastered the habits needed to fulfill them.

Chapter Seven

ψ

SEVEN PLUS SEVEN CORPORATE RESPONSIBILITIES

> While we were once perceived as simply providing services, selling products, and employing people, business now shares in much of the responsibility for our global quality of life. Successful companies will handle this heightened sense of responsibility quite naturally, if not always immediately. I say this not because successful business leaders are altruistic at heart. I can assure you, many are not. I say it because they will demand that their companies remain intensely focused on the needs of their customers and consumers.
>
> —*Roberto C. Goizueta, The Coca-Cola Company*

The virtues classical and modern considered in the previous two chapters strengthen women and men to meet moral responsibilities. Business in particular is a morally serious calling. Women and men of virtue are needed to fulfill it. They face a great many moral responsibilities.

It may help to divide these responsibilities into two different sets. The second set will easily be recognized as "ethics," since the source of their authority comes from outside business—from religious conviction, moral traditions, humane principles, and human rights commitments.

The first set consists of the moral requirements necessary for business success. These are the virtues necessary for building a good business. Alas, these are not always recognized as ethical in their own right. One way to see that they are ethical is to ask yourself what happens when they are violated. If you think earning a profit is a morally neutral rather than morally good way to acquit a responsibility, would you hold that deliberately running losses is ethical—particularly if it's with someone else's money?

The fact that certain actions make a business successful does not disqualify them from being morally good. Too many analysts neglect a basic point: simply to succeed in business imposes remarkable moral responsibilities. Humble as these are, they should be pocketed, taken note of, and given the modest praise that they deserve. Not to have these virtues is to be in a sorry state indeed.

MEDIATING STRUCTURES, CIVIL SOCIETY

Viewed in the long run of history, the business corporation is a fascinating institution. It is a social institution but independent of the state. Its legal existence is transgenerational. It goes on even when its progenitors die, and it may endure across many generations.

Its members come to it voluntarily. They do not give it their entire commitment or the complete energies of life. It is not what Erving Goffman referred to as a "total institution." But they may well commit more sustained time and energy to it than to any other institution of their lives, sometimes including their families.

The business corporation is also a mediating structure, that is, a social institution larger than the individuals who make it up but smaller than the state. An institution both voluntary and private, it stands between the individual and the state and is, perhaps (after the family), the crucial institution of civil society.

Civil society is composed of all those associations, freely chosen or natural (such as the family), through which citizens practice self-government independent of the state. Through the institutions of civil society and its mediating structures, citizens pursue their own affairs, accomplish their social purposes, and enrich the texture of their common life. Civil society is a larger, more basic, and more vital component of social life and the common good than the state is. The state is a servant of civil society. This is caught in Lincoln's classic phrase: "government of the people, by the people, and for the people."

The private business corporation is a necessary (but not sufficient) condition for the success of democracy. This insight is one of the crowning achievements of this nation's founders, who inherited parts of it from Montesquieu. They reasoned that democracy would be safer if built upon the commercial and industrial classes than if built upon the military, aristocratic, priestly, or landed classes.

Furthermore, the founders saw in commerce and manufacture essential keys to economic prosperity. In Article I, section 8 of the Constitution, they looked to the private business corporation for the advancement of the arts and practical sciences—they looked to invention and discovery—and saw in ideas a new form of property far more significant than land.

Only in this one place in the body of the Constitution did the founders use the word *right*, to protect the "right" of authors and inventors to the fruit of their original ideas. In mind, they saw, lies the primary cause of the wealth of nations. To genius of mind they added, as Lincoln admiringly noted, the "fuel of interest." To mind they gave incentives and, later, in the land grant college act, institutional support—the research of an entire array of state-funded universities.

One of the most striking features of early American life, according to Tocqueville, was the delight Americans took in forming associations, in cooperation, and in teamwork. (It is little wonder that the only sports later to attract universal acclaim in the United States were team sports—baseball, football, and basketball.) A major preoccupation of the early centuries was building communities—entire cities where none before had existed. This entailed learning to work together under private auspices, while keeping the state both as weak and as strong as is consistent with self-government.

In this climate, the private business corporation became a prime model of public association, common motivation, mutual dedication, widespread optimism, and the "can do" spirit. "The impossible takes a little longer" is the sort of motto that members of enterprising institutions like to exchange. (Professors, with their professional interest in ambiguity, have always shown discomfort in the face of the rhetoric of business corporations, with their emphasis on getting past ambiguity in order to act successfully. Typically, the temperaments of the professor and the businessman diverge—and the two tend toward genial enmity, one to the other.)

Despite its obvious importance, until recently it has been difficult to find theological or religious writing on the business corporation that meets two conditions: that it is not positively hostile to business and is not merely patronizing, but fair and sympathetic.

As we have seen, the encyclical *Centesimus Annus* (1991) of Pope John Paul II meets this test. We may recall the last lines from a passage cited in part earlier:

The purpose of a business firm is not simply to make a profit, but is to be found in *its very existence as a community of persons* who in various ways are endeavoring to satisfy their basic needs and who form a particular group *at the service of the whole of society*. Profit is a regulator of the life of a business, but it is not the only one; *other human and moral factors must also be considered*, which in the long term are at least equally important for the life of a business. [Emphasis added.]

The private business corporation is an extraordinary institution. It is a practical model for the Christian church to reflect on, "carefully and favorably." The corporation is not a church, not a state, not a welfare agency, not a family. A corporation is an economic association with specific and limited responsibilities.

In this light, seven corporate responsibilities may be said to constitute its primary moral duty. These are the responsibilities internal to it, which must be met simply for it to be a success in doing what it was founded to do. By analogy, schools must meet certain responsibilities to succeed in their proper task of educating the young. We call such schools good schools and such businesses "good" businesses. This sense of the word *good* is freighted with both worldly and moral content.

SEVEN INTERNAL RESPONSIBILITIES

Happy is it for men to be in a situation in which, while their passions inspire in them the thought of being wicked, it is nevertheless, to their interest not to be.
—*Montesquieu*

✧

Some who work in the field of business ethics were trained first in ethics, with a liberal arts background, and tend to think of business corporations as morally naked, unless hung with baubles and jewels from ethics to disguise that nakedness. They see no ethical dimensions inherent in business activities.

As a consequence, a certain dualism appears in many discussions within business ethics. On the one side is business. On the other side are all those other responsibilities that business needs to add on in order to be, or to appear to be, ethical. This is a patronizing and false outlook.

To make the same point by an alternate path: Parents sometimes try to impose on one of their children an ideal of behavior appropriate to another of their children. This often ends up hurting the second child. It might have been better to listen for what is distinctive in that child. Perhaps the lifetime ideal of that child is different from that of their other children—different even from their own—yet altogether proper to that child. It may be wrong to impose on one child ideals that worked very well for another. Similarly, it is wrong to impose aristocratic or socialist ideals on business. It is destructive to impose a social democratic framework on a system that has a different (I think, better) aim.

A business corporation is not a church; not a state; not a welfare agency; not (except rarely) a religious association; not a political association. It is not a "total institution." Thus, it is of considerable importance to discern, first of all, the moral ideals inherent in business as business.

Business is an economic association which, simply by being what it is, serves the common good of the community in several ways. Accordingly, among the corporate responsibilities of business that spring from its own nature are at least these seven:

1. *To satisfy customers with goods and services of real value.* This virtue is not so easy to practice as it seems. Some three out of five new businesses fail—perhaps because the conception their founders have concerning how to serve the customer is not sufficiently realistic, either in its conception or its execution. Like other acts of freedom, launching a new business is in the beginning an act of faith; one has to trust one's instincts

and one's vision and hope that these are well enough grounded
to build success. It is the customers who, in the end, decide.
One set of responsibilities assumed by a business is to its customers. These responsibilities have moral content.

2. *Make a reasonable return on the funds entrusted to the business corporation by its investors*. It is more practical to think of
this responsibility in the second place rather than in the first,
where some writers place it, because only if the first is satisfied
will the second be met. Milton Friedman has made the classic
case for this fundamental social responsibility. I agree with him
in stressing how basic it is but would place it also in the context
of other responsibilities. Friedman's classic statement is:

> The view has been gaining widespread acceptance that corpo-
> rate officials and labor leaders have a "social responsibility"
> that goes beyond serving the interest of their stockholders or
> their members. This view shows a fundamental misconception
> of the character and nature of a free economy. In such an
> economy, there is one and only one social responsibility of
> business—to use its resources and engage in activities
> designed to increase its profits so long as it stays within the
> rules of the game, which is to say, engages in open and free
> competition, without deception or fraud. Similarly, the "social
> responsibility" of labor leaders is to serve the interests of the
> members of their unions. It is the responsibility of the rest of
> us to establish a framework of law such that an individual in
> pursuing his own interest is, to quote Adam Smith again, "led
> by an invisible hand to promote an end which was no part of
> his intention. Nor is it always the worse for the society that it
> was no part of it. By pursuing his own interest, he frequently
> promotes that of the society more effectually than when he
> really intends to promote it. I have never known much good
> done by those who affected to trade for the public good." Few
> trends could so thoroughly undermine the very foundations of
> our free society as the acceptance by corporate officials of a

social responsibility other than to make as much money for their stockholders as possible. This is a fundamentally subversive doctrine.

Note that Friedman's own definition includes a fairly extensive range of moral responsibilities, such as maintaining open and free competition, establishing a framework of the rule of law, avoiding deception and fraud, and exemplifying fair play within the rules of the game. This is altogether no small moral agenda.

So, again, it turns out that even a narrow conception of the purposes of business includes a high level of moral performance found in only a few existing cultures. In most others, moral laxity and corruption of one sort or another are rife.

3. *To create new wealth.* This is no small responsibility. If the business corporation does not meet it, who else in society will?

Probably more than a third of working Americans receive their salaries from nonprofit institutions, which themselves receive their funding from the benefactions of others. These in the end usually derive from the wealth created by business corporations. Roberto Goizueta, Chairman and C.E.O. of Coca Cola, puts this very well:

> [Given that] billions of shares of publicly-held companies are owned by foundations, universities and the like, one should never forget the multiplier effect in the world of philanthropy, and the benefit to society, that each dollar increase in the value of those shares brings about. If a foundation owns, let's say, 50 million shares of Coca-Cola stock, for each dollar that our stock price increases, that foundation will be required to give out an additional $2.5 million.

From this new wealth, too, firms pay a return to investors (in addition to protecting their principal). From this new wealth, provision must also be made for the future, including a fund to underwrite all those failed projects that are certain to happen along the way.

If a company is not creating new wealth, it is spinning its wheels or going into debt or consuming its seed corn; such processes are self-destructive.

Finally, the steady, incremental creation of new wealth is the road to what Adam Smith called "universal opulence." He defined that as the condition in which the real wages of workers keep growing over time, until the poor live at a level that in 1776 even kings and dukes did not enjoy.

4. *To create new jobs.* It is better to teach a man how to fish than to give him a fish, and in the same way it is far better to generate enough jobs for all willing citizens rather than to provide government grants that keep them permanently dependent, in the condition of serfs.

The creation of opportunity is one of the great social responsibilities for whose accomplishment democracies look to business corporations, and in particular to new entrants into the field. The rate of small business formation is usually a very good index of the general health of society—not only its economic health but also its morale, hopefulness, and spirit of generosity toward others.

When economic horizons close down and large masses of people are unemployed, divisive and self-destructive passions such as envy, leveling, and *ressentiment* fester and multiply. In South America, for example, where there are nearly 110 million persons fifteen years old and under, youngsters enter the labor force cohort by cohort with every year that passes, looking for employment, but with little employment to be found. In the future, surely there will be fewer agricultural workers in Latin America and perhaps even fewer working in large industrial factories. Unless there is a rapid expansion of the small business sector, with firms employing from two or three to one hundred workers, it is not easy to see how economic health will come to Latin America.

You cannot create employees without creating employers. Like other societies, Latin America will have to look to its small business sector for any realistic hope of liberating the poor.

Anyone who has enough imagination to generate new jobs should.

5. *To defeat envy through generating upward mobility and putting empirical ground under the conviction that hard work and talent are fairly rewarded.* As we have seen, the founders of the American republic recognized that most other republics in history had failed and that the reason they failed was envy: the envy of one faction for another, one family for another, one clan for another, or of the poor toward the rich. Envy is so pervasive among the human race that in the Ten Commandments, under the name "covetousness," God forbade it seven times. If a republic is to have a long life, it must defeat envy.

The best way to do this is to generate economic growth through as many diverse industries and economic initiatives as possible, so that every family has the realistic possibility of seeing its economic condition improve within the next three or four years. Poor families do not ask for paradise, but they do want to see tangible signs of improvement over time. When such horizons are open, people do not compare their condition with that of their neighbors; rather, they compare their own position today with where they hope to be in three or four years. They give no ground to envy.

A realistic hope of a better future is essential to the poor, and this hope is made realistic only through the provision of universal chances for upward mobility. Only then can people see that hard work, goodwill, ingenuity, and talent pay off. When people lose their faith in this possibility, cynicism soon follows.

For such reasons, a dynamic economy is a necessary

(although not sufficient) condition for the survival and success of democracy. If they do not see real improvement in their economic conditions, people in the formerly communist countries of Central Europe, for example, are not likely to be satisfied merely with the opportunity to vote every two years.

Businesses should avoid fomenting envy; they can do so by supplying employees with opportunities and incentives. In addition, people in business should avoid some things that are otherwise innocent in themselves. Conspicuous privilege, ostentation, and other forms of behavior, even when not necessarily wrong, typically provoke envy. Unusually large salaries or bonuses, even if justified by competition in a free and open market (since high talent of certain kinds is extremely rare), may offer demagogues fertile ground on which to scatter the seeds of envy. It is wise to take precautions against these eventualities.

6. *To promote invention, ingenuity, and in general, "progress in the arts and useful sciences"* (Article I, Section 8, U.S. Constitution). The heart of capitalism is *caput*: the human mind, human invention, human enterprise. Pope John Paul II puts it well: "Indeed, besides the earth, man's principal resource is *man himself*." And again: "Today the decisive factor is increasingly *man himself*; that is, his knowledge, especially his scientific knowledge, his capacity for interrelated and compact organization, as well as his ability to perceive the needs of others, and to satisfy them." The great social matrix of such invention, discovery, and ingenuity is the business corporation.

The Constitution gives an incentive to discover new practical ideas and to bring them to the realistic service of one's neighbors. Perhaps no other practical device in history has so revolutionized the daily conditions of life. It has brought about a higher level of the common good than any people ever experienced before.

As we have seen, creativity is a cardinal virtue of business life. Firms that blunt the creative edge of their employees violate the image of God in them—and stultify themselves.

7. *To diversify the interests of the republic.* One of the least observed functions of the business corporation is to concretize the economic loyalties of citizens and to sort out their practical knowledge into diverse sectors of life. The interests of road builders are not those of canal builders, or of builders of railroads, or of airline companies. The sheer dynamism of economic invention makes far less probable the coalescing of a simple majority, which could act as a tyrant to minorities. The economic interests of some citizens are, in an important sense, at cross-purposes with the economic interests of others, and this is crucial to preventing the tyranny of a majority.

In cities, towns, and states, accordingly, it is wise for civic leaders to promote a healthy diversity of business interests. It is also sound practice for business leaders to encourage their employees to be as entrepreneurial as possible, even if they end up going into business for themselves. Such events are signs of business as well as social health.

All seven of these economic responsibilities need to be met by a nation's business corporations. All seven are crucial to the health of the state and, more important, to the health of civil society, which is the master social reality.

But there are also other responsibilities, inherent not so much in business qua business as in the convictions of its practitioners.

SEVEN RESPONSIBILITIES
FROM OUTSIDE BUSINESS

Romano Guardini once wrote that you should be able to tell a Catholic even from the way he climbs a tree. He meant that the cult of the Catholic church, like that of all other great religions, is culture forming. The liturgy is intended to inspire a distinctive style of life. *To labor is to pray*. Our callings in the world are intended to be, in the doing of them, ways of praying. It is not so much that we should pray as we work as that we should intend our work as a wordless prayer.

Therefore, while the business corporation has a set of inherent responsibilities, proper to itself, these do not exhaust the responsibilities of Christians or Jews whose vocation calls them to the business world. Without intending to be exhaustive, and in a kind of shorthand, one might discern seven further sets of moral responsibilities proper to the business worker as Christian or Jew. (In most matters affecting business, it turns out, the biblical imperatives weighing on Jews and Christians are similar.) I have taken pains to state them in a way that shows their relevance to business and makes them analogously compelling to those who are not Jewish or Christian. In this second set of responsibilities, as in the first set, I list but seven:

1. *To establish within the firm a sense of community and respect for the dignity of persons*, thus shaping within the firm a culture that fosters the three cardinal virtues of business and other virtues. This also means fostering respect for the standards, discipline, motivation, and teamwork that brings out the best in people, encourages their moral and intellectual growth, and helps them gain a sense of high achievement and personal fulfillment.

As Ellen Marram, president of Seagram's Beverage Group, puts it: "While growing one's business is important, I think it's equally important to grow one's employees. Many of the people I've worked with in the past have gone on to run other divisions and companies, and I feel good about any contribution I may have made to their learning and development. It's a role I take seriously."

2. *To protect the political soil of liberty.* Since free business corporations are permitted to operate freely only in a minority of countries on this earth, those involved in business must come to see how fragile their activities are; they can be crushed by war, revolution, tyranny, and anarchy. Most people on earth today, like most others in history, have suffered from such devastations. Many individuals have rarely experienced the peace, stability, and institutional environment that supports the daily activities and long-term hopes of business. Some have never experienced them.

Businesses are plants that do not grow in just any soil; they depend on specific sorts of political environments. People in business therefore have a responsibility to be watchful over their political society, even as a matter of survival. It is no accident that they love liberty as ardently as any others in history and, indeed, have often been forerunners of free societies.

Since the survival of business depends on the survival of free institutions, the responsibilities of people in business include the need to build majorities well informed about the principles of the free society.

A look at the top 20 percent of American society—its elite, defined in terms of income, education, and status (professionals, managers, the self-employed)—shows that our elite is roughly divided into two parts. Call one part the "Old Elite," whose income and status depend on the expansion of the private sector, particularly the business sector. Describe as the "New Class" those who see their own income, power, and status as dependent on the expansion of the state. These two rivals vie for the allegiance of a democratic majority.

A society simultaneously democratic and capitalist benefits

when these two perennial rivals are of roughly equal strength, so that the free political system and the free economic system are in healthy equilibrium. (Given the tendency of the state to amass power and even coercive force, however, a society is probably closer to healthy equilibrium when at least a slight majority favors economic liberty.)

Businesses should encourage their employees, retirees, and shareholders to take political ideas and policy issues seriously, to participate in electoral campaigns, and to vote.

3. *To exemplify respect for law*. Business cannot survive without the rule of law. Long-term contracts depend for their fulfillment on respect for law. Often in America we take the rule of law for granted and hardly appreciate how fragile it may be. In any case, hardly any other institution is so much at risk as the business corporation, and hardly any is so dependent on the reliability, speed, and efficiency of the daily operation of the rule of law. Thus it is doubly scandalous for people in business to break the law. It is wrong in itself, and it is also suicidal, since to the extent that the law falls into disrespect, the life of corporations is rendered insecure, if not impossible.

4. *Social justice*. Friedrich Hayek pointed out that as most people use it, the term *social justice* is incoherent. They say they are talking about a "virtue" (a characteristic habit of a person), but then they describe a condition of society, for which no one person is responsible. By contrast, the virtue of social justice is a virtue highly important to business, in this way: Business is a crucial (perhaps *the* crucial) institution of civil society. Civil society (and business, too) depends on the rule of law, on the one side, and on a potent set of moral and cultural institutions, on the other. For its own well-being and survival, business therefore depends on its personnel being active in civil society: in politics, the law, churches, the arts, charitable works, and other civic

activities. That is why, typically, businesses encourage their employees to practice social action, to volunteer for civic activities, and to be good citizens in the local community.

The essence of social justice is to look with the eyes of justice ("give to each his due") at the present condition of society; to reflect with others about what needs to be done to improve things; and to act with others in practical, effective ways to move toward that goal. In this sense, social justice has two aspects. First, it is a habit (disposition, inclination) inherent in individual persons, and thus truly the *virtue* of social justice. Second, its *social* character is shown in two ways: its aim is to improve some aspect of society, and its characteristic form of action is to organize others or at least to work jointly with others toward that aim. In both respects, this virtue carries the self into involvement with others for the sake of the human city and is thus truly *social* justice.

Hayek himself was a great practitioner of this virtue. He dedicated himself to developing sound realistic ideas concerning the constitution of the good society. He started many organizations designed to improve society both by advancing sound ideals for society and by urging practical steps in the direction of those ideals.

It goes without saying that the first focus of employees and managers of a business might be how to make their company more humane ("Give each his due" as creator, person of dignity, and vital member of the corporate community). Like other forms of justice and love, social justice begins at home. Yet its ultimate focus is on the whole of the human city: the civilization of freedom, justice, and mutual respect.

5.   *To communicate often and fully with their investors, shareholders, pensioners, customers, and employees.* A business firm represents ever-widening circles of people, and part of its civic responsibility (and much to its long-term advantage) is to

keep all of them informed about its purposes, needs, risks, dangers, and opportunities. In a democratic society, the corporation needs the support of a great many citizens and is of itself—especially over against the omnivorous administrative state of the late twentieth century—exceedingly fragile.

This responsibility rests particularly on people of business in nondemocratic and newly democratic lands. In South Korea, Chile, Poland, the Czech Republic, and many other lands, it is crucial for business leaders not to neglect their responsibilities toward democracy. The same is true for American firms overseas.

Such networks of people can do much to help the poor and needy of the world (see chapter 9).

6.   *To contribute to making its own habitat, the surrounding society, a better place.* It is much to the advantage of the business firm that the republican experiment in self-government succeed. And this project of self-government requires an active private sector as an alternative to the state. The business firm therefore has a responsibility to become a leader in civil society. To this end, it should contribute to the good fortune of other mediating structures in the private sector, whether in areas such as education and the arts, healthful activities for youth, the environment, care for the elderly, new initiatives to meet the needs of the homeless and the poor, and other such activities. The business corporation cannot take primary responsibility in this area; it is not, in itself, a welfare organization. Nevertheless, it does well to nurture the networks of civil society and to strengthen those of its allies who provide an alternative to government.

During 1994, some 89 million U.S. citizens over the age of eighteen dedicated an average of 4.5 hours per week to voluntary activities in such projects as these. It is a responsibility that business owes to the project of self-government—citizens doing for themselves, not relying on government—to encourage their own constituencies to participate in civil life.

Government is not the enemy of business or of the citizens. On the other hand, historically, it has been a fertile source of tyranny, corruption, the abuse of rights, and plain arrogance of power. The alternative to excessive reliance on the state is self-government: sustained and systematic voluntary activities. This capacity for self-government is precisely what "the republican experiment" of the United States is testing: Can it take the pressure—or must the nation relapse, like others, into statism?

7. *To protect the moral ecology of freedom*. In many countries, the media (especially television) are paid for and controlled by government. In fully free societies, commercial sponsors pay for television time. Although I am reluctant to propose that they should control (have a censor's power over) program content, such sponsors do control their own advertising—and they also have responsibility for the content their advertising budgets pay for. Most executives, it appears, have not accepted responsibility for the ecology of the television environment.

A visitor from a distant continent who looked at American television for a week might be amazed by its kaleidoscope of images, narratives, symbols, and assumptions about the nature of reality. These would also have shocked our great-grandparents; they often enough shock *us*.

One striking feature of the advertising as well as of the surrounding prime-time and afternoon domestic shows is their *ir*religiousness, their worldliness, their lack of any sense of eternal life. This aspect of television is far out of accord with the history of American culture. Recall the unself-conscious piety found in Civil War letters. It is also remarkably out of touch with the religious lives of most Americans today, who, when tragedy strikes, as well as success (football players kneeling down to express gratitude after completing a great play), turn first to God. The commercials—particularly the beer, automobile, and fragrance commercials—share as much in this aggressive worldliness (this virtual *anti*religiousness) as the programs they accompany.

Yet this characteristic worldliness is tame compared to the aggressive animal-like sexuality and brutal violence that form the lure of television's excitement and innuendo. By their products, the creators of the television world would seem to do their work with a constant leer. Naturally, the public is susceptible to this constant playing to their prurient interests. It assaults us in our own homes; it is amiable; it is free; and part of our nature does respond to it—the least noble, most beastly part of our nature. We often consent to it even when cheapened by it. "Giving the public what it wants" is here no boasting matter. It is, in fact, a form of prostitution.

Even in announcing his retirement from the U.S. Senate, the sober and prudent Sam Nunn (D, Georgia) could not forebear issuing a stark challenge to corporate executives:

> Too many parents who are struggling to provide their children with basic needs have no way to protect them from street violence and drugs. If America is to remain the greatest country on earth, our children must come first. . . . Too many executives are spending too many corporate dollars paying for television programs that bombard our homes with sex and violence—not thinking or caring about the effect of this bombardment on our children and our nation's future.
>
> Too many of us as citizens sit by passively while this bombardment takes place.
>
> We are reaping the harvest from this combination of conditions in soaring rates of child abuse, drug abuse, teenage pregnancies, abortions and unprecedented levels of crime and violence.

In the past, corporate executives thought their role in advertising and sponsorship to be quite limited. In fact, however, it is far more extensive than they thought. They are rightly being blamed for the ethos reflected through the television sets in the nation's homes.

It is shocking, for example, that in the television series most watched by global audiences, "Dallas," the most murderous, lying, double-dealing, cheating, wife-swapping cads on the shows are usually businessmen, *and that this slander on the business community has been produced and paid for by business sponsors*. Businessmen are the first minority not only to allow their moral reputation to be systematically dragged through the mud every night but also to pay for the privilege.

All around the world, the major existing threat to free markets and democracy at the end of the twentieth century springs from the systematic corruption of popular culture. Systemic moral decline undermines the capacity of peoples for self-government.

Corporate executives have grave responsibilities to supervise their advertising departments far more rigorously than they now do, discerning whether their product weakens in the public mind the virtues on which the free society depends.

SPECIAL BUSINESS CODES

In the previous chapter, we noted the blizzard of contingencies faced by business leaders as new developments and market changes swirl around them. Important events tend to happen suddenly. You go to the office after a normal speedy breakfast and—*bam*! an emergency arrives on the desk. There isn't much time to think about what to do.

This is the way it was at Johnson & Johnson (J&J) several years ago, when an unprecedented scare hit its most popular product, Tylenol. A news flash hit the home office like a blue lightning bolt: seven people dead in Chicago. Someone had apparently tampered with Tylenol bottles, lacing some capsules with cyanide. Early investigation suggested the cause was neither an employee nor a manufacturing site. It was tampering, by parties unknown. There were no reported cases in any other location.

Virtually without hesitation, top executives at J&J immediately ordered the withdrawal of all Tylenol capsules from the entire U.S. market, although all the deaths occurred only in the Chicago area. They also assigned twenty-five hundred personnel to an all-out communication effort to alert the public to the problem, to prevent any further incidents. The cost of removing the product amounted to $100 million. The *Washington Post* wrote of the crisis that "Johnson & Johnson has succeeded in portraying itself to the public as a company willing to do what's right, regardless of cost." But J&J not only portrayed itself that way. That's the way it acted. It was in no position to dictate the portrayal the media would give to its actions. It just did the right thing, and let the chips fall. One hundred million dollars worth.

Business doesn't always act that way. Within a few days of the Tylenol crisis—this was in 1982—Bristol-Myers was hit by a similar news flash: Excedrin tablets had been tampered with in the Denver area. Later describing himself as "a cautious manager who likes to count things down to the last bean," the Bristol-Myers chairman Richard Gelb also acted quickly but recalled Excedrin tablets only from the Denver area, not (as J&J had done) from the whole country. Unlike J&J, he launched no campaign to warn the public. Gelb was quick to tell the business press that the Excedrin crisis would affect company earnings negatively, even if the announcement added to downward pressure on the stock.

One difference between the speed and thoroughness of the response in these two cases is especially instructive. When emergencies erupt in such startling rapidity, it is almost impossible to think. Information is fragmentary. Sorting reliable from unreliable detail is difficult. Direct economic and other consequences of each public move are staggering, in all directions. Confusion paralyzes the brain.

Here a preexisting company code is a godsend. Executives do not have to establish a new company policy or worry about defending themselves later before company trustees. They can turn to the code for instant guidance. Johnson & Johnson's founder, R. W. Johnson, Jr., had penned a credo for the company in 1943 that had often been cited as precedent for tactical decisions. In the Tylenol crisis thirty-nine years later, the credo was like a rock, once again giving executives instant assurance.

Bristol-Myers did not have anything so formal. Mr. Gelb was on his own.

Nor was 1982 the only time that the credo helped J&J through a crisis. One of the company's great all-time products is baby oil. At a time when the risks of skin cancer from sunlight were not known except in a few circles in research medicine, the company launched an advertising campaign for Johnson & Johnson Baby Oil as a way to help babies get a tan in the sun. Seeing the ad, a medical friend of a J&J executive mentioned new research that said tanning might be harmful. He thought exposure to the sun while using baby oil might be even worse. J&J investigated, confirmed the worry, and immediately canceled the advertising campaign. "It simply would be wrong," said the executive who made the decision. The credo backed him up.

For such reasons, it might be useful to reprint the Johnson & Johnson Credo here. It is widely studied in business schools—made fun of sometimes, but nevertheless studied. (Ethical codes always have a ring to them that prompts irreverence.) This code's very abstractness—written in 1943 to be relevant under unforeseen circumstances decades later—lends it a stilted air. Yet it has proved its worth in times of crisis. The first three lines laid out everything necessary to meet the Tylenol crisis.

Our Credo

We believe that our first responsibility is to the doctors, nurses, hospitals, mothers, and all others who use our products. Our products must always be of the highest quality. We must constantly strive to reduce the cost of these products. Our orders must be promptly and accurately filled. Our dealers must make a fair profit.

Our second responsibility is to those who work with us—the men and women in our plants and offices. They must have a sense of security in their jobs. Wages must be fair and adequate, management just, hours reasonable, and working conditions clean and orderly. Employees should have an organized system for suggestions and complaints. Supervisors and department heads must be qualified and fair-minded. There must be opportunity for advancement for those qualified and each person must be considered an individual standing on his own dignity and merit.

Our third responsibility is to our management. Our executives must be persons of talent, education, experience, and ability. They must be persons of common sense and full understanding.

Our fourth responsibility is to the communities in which we live. We must be a good citizen—support good works and charity, and bear our fair share of taxes. We must maintain in good order the property we are privileged to use.

We must participate in promotion of civic improvement, health, education and good government, and acquaint the community with our activities.

✧

Our fifth and last responsibility is to our stockholders. Business must make a sound profit. Reserves must be created, research must be carried on, adventurous programs developed, and mistakes paid for. Adverse times must be provided for, adequate taxes paid, new machines purchased, new plants built, new products launched, and new sales plans developed. We must experiment with new ideas. When these things have been done the stockholder should receive a fair return. We are determined with the help of God's grace to fulfill these obligations to the best of our ability.

✧

Johnson & Johnson and Bristol-Myers are not the only companies to have faced crises. Procter & Gamble also faced one, this time having to deal with what they had thought was a triumphantly superior product.

To the benefit of succeeding generations of executives, Procter & Gamble had a moral tradition that was the functional equivalent to J&J's credo. Here's what happened, according to John Pepper, president of Procter & Gamble, some years after the crisis:

> P&G faced a very difficult situation in the early 1980s on Rely Tampons, a feminine hygiene product. It was during this period that an outbreak occurred of a very serious disease called Toxic Shock Syndrome. In the worst cases, it could be fatal. In some studies, there appeared to be at least a circumstantial association with the use of tampons, including Rely.

We had launched Rely two years before. It had very quickly become the #1 brand on the market. We had done a great deal of scientific testing ourselves, and with the help of renowned outside scientists, and we had every indication the product was safe to use.

Yet, the problem was real and there was at least a circumstantial association with the use of our own and other products. What were we to do?

I'll always remember how our Chief Executive Officer, Ed Harness, made the decision. He assembled leaders from the different disciplines in his office and he asked a simple straightforward question: "Can you give me absolute assurance that there is no involvement of our product in this disease which could lead to serious harm to the consumer?"

On the one hand, our scientists said there was absolutely no indication that Rely was involved in these tragic deaths. On the other hand, testing did not exist to categorically eliminate the possibility that there was some involvement.

The answer was clear. Ed Harness made his decision on the spot. He didn't wait for additional studies. He didn't delay until the public pressure forced him to act. Instead, he decided to withdraw Rely from the market—immediately—across the nation. He knew the costs would be high—almost $100 million. But the decision was an easy one.

Among those for whom business is a moral or religious calling, this is the way they wish they would act if need arises. Companies that cut corners, or waffle morally, shame their profession.

A MORAL INSTITUTION

The business corporation is in its essence a moral institution. It imposes some moral obligations that are inherent in its own ends, structure, and modes of operation. Other moral obligations fall upon it through the moral and religious commitments of its members. Thus, those who labor within the business corporation have many moral responsibilities and a richly various moral agenda, of which the fourteen responsibilities mentioned here are basic but not exhaustive.

Those who do not allow that business is a moral institution injure themselves twice over. First, they fall prey to a common aristocratic prejudice. Second, since a healthy capitalist economy is a necessary condition for the success of democracy, they diminish the prospects of the free society.

The most important responsibility of the woman or man of business, however, is highly personal. "What does it profit a man if he gains the whole world and suffers the loss of his soul?" (Mark 8:36) The first concern of ethical reflection is how one's actions affect one's own soul.

Long ago, Aristotle pointed out that the proper focus of ethical reflection falls upon those actions that change our own nature—that establish in us a "second nature." Ethics itself is a calling; it calls us to change our way of life for the long term. It means grounding ourselves in new habits. It means building—slowly, patiently, deeply—our own character. It means choosing wisely among the virtues we build up in ourselves. It means identifying the vices most difficult for us to resist—the ones we secretly hate to part with.

Both democracy and capitalism depend on certain specific virtues, such as creativity, building community (civic spirit), and practical realism. Both regimes (political and economic) disdain the passivity imposed by socialism; both call forth spirited action. They depend on self-starters with a strong sense of personal responsibility and civic cooperation. Because of the hazards and dangers always threatening republican self-governance, both regimes induce a spirit of thanksgiving.

In sum, business has many responsibilities to the moral ecology of our nation, and especially to the culture of virtue. It has been wrong—devastatingly wrong—for advertisers *in the name of business* to promote assaults on traditional virtues. These are the muscles, ligaments, sinews of the free society. Cut them, and you have paralyzed liberty.

Chapter Eight

❦

BUSINESS AND HUMAN RIGHTS

American firms' normal business procedures incorporate a sort of grassroots meritocracy and openness not found in many host-country companies. U.S. and Western multinationals reward employees based on performance, not out of patronage or other non-professional consider-ations. They tend to treat local unions respectfully, demonstrating to populations lacking in basic freedoms that representation and negotiation are concepts that can work. Multinationals emphasize training and work-place benefits, further reinforcing the idea that every individual has intrinsic potential and human dignity. . . . In addition, we should remember that not all business decisions are made as a result of cost-benefit analyses. Managers are people, too; given several sound business options, there is no reason why they will not choose the one that makes a human situation better.

—Harvard Professor Debora L. Spar

In China in 1994 an American citizen, Harry Wu, identified 1,168 prison labor camps in which hundreds of thousands of political prisoners were being "reeducated" and often tortured. The products made by such prisoners were often being offered to—and purchased by—businesses in the United States. When this fact came to public notice, much scandal ensued, and several companies withdrew from prior arrangements in considerable embarrassment.

Chinese officials often demand that other American businesses in China report to them regarding certain private behaviors of their Chinese employees, for example, their political opinions and childbearing habits. (More than one child per family is forbidden.) Sometimes governments (e.g., those of Burma, Vietnam, and Sri Lanka) demand that Western business leaders stick to business and raise no questions about human rights practices.

Imagine the surprise and contempt that courses through tyrants when corporate leaders buckle under to them, abandon their own moral standards, and make themselves complacent in evil. That is the primrose path down which the system of natural liberty is dragged toward its befoulment.

It is bad enough for a firm to betray itself. Why need it betray the best ideals its nation stands for?

In such cases, what are the responsibilities of business leaders?

The main justification for businesses opening operations in totalitarian and authoritarian regimes is called "constructive engagement" and is based on wedge theory. Capitalist practices, runs the theory, bring contact with the ideas and practices of the free societies, generate the economic growth that gives political confidence to a rising middle class, and raise up successful business leaders who come to represent a political alternative to military or party leaders. In short, capitalist firms wedge a democratic camel's nose under the authoritarian tent.

There is no doubt that this strategy has worked in the past. Experience has verified the hypothesis that capitalist institutions are a necessary (but not sufficient) condition for the emergence and success of democratic regimes. A successful democratic revolution depends on the growth of a confident middle class and the emergence of proven civilian leaders. It depends on the growth of civil society, that is, on a whole range of nongovernmental associations, anchored in the real possibilities opened up by a growing economy. It depends on the growth of property rights, if not yet in law, at least in practice. In such matters, practice often precedes law. As the motto of the University of Pennsylvania puts it: *Leges sine moribus vanae*: Apart from established practices, laws are empty.

Yet the strategy of constructive engagement may sometimes ask too little of corporations and sell short their true revolutionary power. Private business corporations are *in themselves* embodiments of practices of human rights. They impart visions of human possibility, and in their own interest promote the rule of law.

Precisely because they carry such dynamic tendencies within them, business corporations insert a wedge of liberty into closed societies by their mere presence.

But that presence need not be, and should not be, passive. Business leaders should not hold back the moral dynamism their firms embody. They have both a long-term and a short-term interest in becoming aggressive in being who they really are, both in narrowly economic dimensions and in the moral dimensions of their corporate existence.

What holds many back is a traditional but demeaning self-image. This traditional self-image tells them that they are not moral beings, only economic animals. This message does not do them justice. It is, in fact, false.

One can easily understand how this self-image arose. When private business corporations began to intrude on public consciousness in the West, toward the end of the eighteenth century, they undermined some of the traditional moral arguments based on the habits and customs of the feudal economy that had governed European (and Asian) life for more than a thousand years.

Traditional moralists defended the old order and upbraided the new. "The poor ye shall always have with you," the old order said, but the new order dreamed of liberating the poor from their immemorial poverty. The moralists of the old order preferred the stasis of the past to the unsettling dynamism of the new.

Further, most (but not all) traditional moralists diagnosed the striving to create new wealth as a sign of avarice and greed. A large majority of artists and intellectuals, accustomed to identifying themselves with the aristocratic order (and to imagining themselves to be "aristocrats of the spirit"), denounced the "dark satanic mills" (William Blake), the nouveaux riches, the entrepreneurs, and the newly appearing industrialists as vulgar and, in the end, evil.

In retaliation, finding so little sympathy among the moralists of church and crown, the early economists began to state their own aims in a language designed to *épater les moralistes*. Although most of the early economists such as Adam Smith and John Stuart Mill were moral philosophers, they found it rhetorically useful in this intellectual combat to ridicule the traditional moralists. They presented them as out of touch, blind to the empirical consequences of their fine moral ideas. Increasingly, they began to define economics as a way of thinking quite different from, even apart from, (traditional) moral thinking. These new economists did not think that they were being immoral or even amoral in their new way of thinking. They plainly thought that their new theories were more moral than those of the moralists who denounced them. They thought that their new theories would do more for the poor, were more in touch with daily reality, and would do more for the common good than all the fine (but hollow) moralizing of the traditionalists.

Annoyed by the moralism and affected righteousness of their critics, the new economists began to abandon moral arguments, surrendering this terrain to (as they judged) hollow moralizers, while claiming for themselves the language of "realism."

The problem with this unfortunate short-cut—whose appeal in the circumstances is understandable—is that, at the end of the day, human beings are moral animals. It is their nature to believe in the goodness of what they are doing. The new economists certainly did. We have only to listen to the classical economists of our own day—Milton Friedman, for example—to detect unmistakable tones of moral seriousness (even a whiff of moral superiority). Moral self-doubt is not something we associate with libertarian economists. But if the tone is highly moral and the self-image that gave rise to that tone is so as well, the language of modern economists is remarkably (and falsely) premoral. At least, modern economics *pretends* to be premoral. It attempts to assume that human beings in their economic activities are "purely" economic, without any "contamination" by moral considerations.

As a rhetorical strategy, we can understand this in the circumstances of intellectual history as it actually unfolded. But it was not strictly necessary. It coincided with a larger intellectual project, the Enlightenment, a willful attempt to reconstruct human thought without reference to God or to the enduring moral standards of the past.

Suppose that *religious* thinkers and other traditional moralists had immediately grasped the new human possibilities first sketched by Adam Ferguson, Francis Hutcheson, Adam Smith, John Stuart Mill, and their colleagues. Suppose that the former had welcomed the latter instead of attacking them as immoralists. Suppose that traditional religious and moral principles had been revised in the light of new knowledge about the new economic possibilities of modernity.

All that, sadly, did not happen. But if it had, the growing compatibility between economic life and religious and moral life that many of us today experience might never have been impeded. It would, instead, have been part of economic thinking from the beginning.

The truth is that we human subjects simultaneously experience ourselves as both economic agents and religious and moral agents. We do not easily compartmentalize our living practice. When we try to do so, we feel the strain, verging on betrayal of one or the other. Moral schizophrenia is not a natural state.

As we have seen, business corporations carry within them certain important moral virtues, such as the principles of creativity and community. They embody subtle filaments of law, custom, habits, practices, and understandings, without which they could not exist, or have permanence across the generations.

Business corporations are crucial institutions of civil society. They are built on foundations of constitutionally recognized rights, such as rights of association, rights to property (including intellectual property), the right to individual economic initiative, and the like.

Business corporations are, in fact, voluntary communities unified by certain tasks to be performed and mutual duties to be met. Most of all, they are unified by the mutual respect that one human being owes another.

Business corporations are dependent on the rule of law and, indeed, on political regimes favorable to their existence and free operation. They also depend on a certain moral ethos embodied, and practiced, by those who participate in them and deal with them. They can be frustrated by systematic moral failures in their own ranks.

They require a high degree of human trust for their own efficient and happy working.

THE TRANSNATIONAL FIRM

> We advise our employees to use a simple test to distinguish between actions that are right and wrong. The test goes as follows: When evaluating the rightness or wrongness of a business action, ask yourself these two questions. Would you be ashamed to describe the full details of this action to your family? Would you be embarrassed to read about it on the front page of your local newspaper? If you answer yes to either one, then your action is probably unethical and possibly illegal. Don't do it!
> —*Richard J. Stegemeier, Unocal*

When a business corporation enters into the horizon of a political regime and moral ethos different from the one in which it has been nurtured, it arrives as a moral institution freighted with its own moral and constitutional imperatives.

Recognizing that societies throughout the world differ dramatically in their political regimes and moral practices, business leaders also recognize that business corporations have certain advantages over political and religious institutions. Unlike the latter, business corporations do not frontally threaten foreign states. Business corporations are, in the British philosopher Michael Oakeshott's felicitous distinction, enterprise associations: task oriented, limited in scope and purpose, not at all totalistic.

Thus, foreign regimes may well see in corporations particular utilities that they desire and particular tasks to be performed, useful to these regimes, and of only modest threat to them. Thereby is established the mutual ground on which constructive engagement rests. Thus also is established the possibility of the wedge.

From the point of view of the participating business corporation itself, the situation is far different. First of all, the corporation will not want its moral reputation tarnished by complicity in the crimes and abuses of human rights that a particular regime may practice. Second, it will certainly wish to keep its moral distance and to maintain its own internal moral standards.

Not being a primarily political association—though it contains within itself a structure of laws and practices deriving from its origin in a quite different political regime—it will not feel the imperative to demand that the foreign regime change its political nature. Yet a transnational firm can hardly help knowing that a change in the direction of respect for human rights and the rule of law—toward the type of regime in which the transnational firm would best be secure and prosper— would be in its own long-term interests.

A world of democracies favorable to capitalist development, living under the rule of law and respecting human rights, is a desideratum devoutly to be wished, from the point of view of both business and the universal human good. Also in the short-term interest of the business corporation, moreover, is fidelity to its own internal moral standards, that is, corporate behavior that wins moral respect from the leaders and people of every land in which the company operates.

"There are certain things," serious corporate leaders will make clear to their colleagues in the field, "that *this* corporation simply does not do. There is no dollar worth making that requires the besmirching of this firm's hard-won moral reputation." A typical public statement of this sort was made by Unocal's chairman (now retired), Richard J. Stegemeier:

> Unocal's policy has always been to operate as a good corporate citizen in full compliance with the law. To the best of our ability, we also try to comply with the spirit as well as with the letter of the law. . . . Our employees . . . are expected to treat others fairly

and with respect, to maintain a safe workplace, to promote a clean environment, and to strive for excellence in all company activities. We like to say: If we can't afford to do it right, then we won't do it at all.

A stern moral posture is likely, ironically, to win the respect of even the most corrupt dictatorship. Such a regime, accustomed to distrusting everyone and everything, is typically glad to know that a particular corporation is as good as its word.

The annals of corporate life contain many examples of such hard-won respect. Even when other firms accept bribes, the firm that does not tends to be remembered, even by those who tried to corrupt it. This firm may lose one or more projects. Yet often enough to make honesty worthwhile, corrupt regimes frequently turn to incorruptible firms for vital and important projects. Top leaders may even see to it that the way is cleared all down the line for such firms to operate in the way in which they are accustomed, since the rulers know that the job will be done well and for an honest (and predictable) price. In the experience of corrupt regimes, reliable moral behavior may seem as rare as it is welcome. Companies that show self-respect win respect. They are likely to gain a steady stream of projects.

MORALITY HAS COSTS

The practical point to be drawn from these reflections is *not* that honesty always pays off; it does not. It often has costs. For moral reasons alone, these costs are worth paying.

But for business reasons, too, a reputation for incorruptibility is a priceless asset. In the world as it is, there are a multitude of competing projects in which such a reputation will tip the balance in the minds of those who award contracts.

In other words, a religious and moral business leader has

plenty of room for doing the right thing and insisting on it throughout the company. People employed by the firm enjoy knowing that they work for a serious, moral association. Foreign rulers who are themselves corrupt can scarcely help paying grudging respect, however unexpected they may find such behavior. Such behavior sows a fertile seed in history.

But there is a stronger point. A concrete case may make it vivid.

According to human rights monitors, one of the cruelest and most corrupt regimes today is the military dictatorship in Burma. Human rights protestors exist in Burma; one of them, Aung San Suu Kyi, for many years under house arrest, won the Nobel Prize for her heroism. What are such activists to think if foreign corporations do business with the dictatorship that so oppresses them *without interceding on their behalf*, at least quietly and steadily? They will surely believe that such firms, and the political economy they represent, have no moral conscience and do not represent a model to which they can aspire.

In short, such a business firm will damage not only its own moral reputation but also that of the system it claims to love. It will commit a triple evil: one against those whose plight it does not lift a finger to alleviate, a second against its own moral well-being, and a third against the regime of liberty it claims to represent. It will damage everything it loves. It will give comfort to the enemies of regimes of liberty, who insist that the cash nexus is the only thing that really counts under the false name of liberty.

A constructive engagement that is wholly passive, in which the company in question lacks the self-confidence to speak up for what it believes in, turns out to be destructive, not constructive.

Moral self-confidence, however, can achieve other results. Consider the Unocal Corporation, which has signed a contract with the government of Burma as a minority investing partner

(Total, a French firm, will be the operator and larger partner) to develop a natural gas field offshore Myanmar. Human rights activists have focused on Unocal, accusing it of entering into an immoral contract with an evil regime. From Unocal's point of view, rooted in long experience in Southeast Asia, the development of this gas field will have beneficial consequences for the people of Burma long after the dictatorship is gone. The activists point out, in rebuttal, that Unocal's existing contract is now the major source of hard currency for the detested regime. They want Unocal to renounce it. Should the company oblige?

That it should do so is far from clear to me.

As it happens, a college chum of mine is manager of government relations at Unocal, and over the years I have discussed this situation with him for hours. I am not in a position to pass judgment on everything involved, but I can say that the people at Unocal have inquisitive and alert minds, are mindful of the full range of their responsibilities in Burma, and have taken many brave initiatives. They are trying hard—and some of the things they are doing may prove helpful to others.

The first thing to note is that Unocal has established a company code, in whose light it wishes to be publicly judged, and it takes this code seriously. This code is published in a 16-page booklet and distributed to every employee, who is required to sign a card stating that he or she has read and understood the code and then to return the card to the appropriate supervisory personnel. As the chairman states, "Unocal's code of business conduct is our bible of business behavior. We take it as seriously as our three-year business plan. In fact, compliance with our code is a condition of employment. Failure to comply is grounds for discipline, including dismissal."

The position of the code that deals with international operations follows. I am not in a position to state that Unocal employees have always followed this code, but if they have not, it is legitimate for the public at large to join the company in condemning them.

STATEMENT OF PRINCIPLES
Unocal's code of conduct for doing business internationally

Meet the highest ethical standards in all of our business activities.

- Conduct business in a way that engenders pride in our employees and respect from the world community.

Treat everyone fairly and with respect.

- Offer equal employment opportunity for all host country nationals, regardless of race, ethnic group, or sex.
- Make sure that a very high percentage of the work force is made up of nationals.
- Train and develop national employees so they have full access to opportunities for professional advancement and positions at higher levels in the organization.

Maintain a safe and healthful workplace.

- As employees, value and protect each other's health and safety as highly as we do our own.

Use local goods and services as much as practical, whenever they're competitive and fit our needs.

Improve the quality of life in the communities where we do business.

- Contribute—and not just economically—to local communities, so that our presence enhances people's lives in long-lasting, meaningful ways.

Protect the environment.

- Take our environmental responsibilities seriously and abide by all environmental laws of our host country, as we do in the United States.

Communicate openly and honestly.

- Maintain our policy of encouraging meaningful dialogue with concerned shareholders, employees, the media, and members of the public.

Be a good corporate citizen and a good friend of the people of our host country.

In Burma, Unocal is clearly in a position to express these moral standards to the government and to advance arguments that might persuade Burma's leaders that abuses of human rights are against its own interests. In fact, Unocal has often done so, quietly but steadily. In this case, Unocal and its partners do not represent solely themselves. Like it or not, they represent a key institution of the free society: the business corporation. In Myanmar, they are the major example of what a capitalist firm truly values and holds dear.

Unocal's behavior, and that of its partners, will either add luster to the ideal of a free society and its economic institutions, as the company recognizes, or discredit that ideal for some time to come. The company accepts this responsibility quite openly.

Without being in Burma myself, and without knowing just who the key personalities are representing Unocal and the government, I cannot judge the human chemistry and the kinds of opportunities for frank speech that currently obtain. But I have inquired and have learned of several different circumstances in which a representative of the company has asked a representative of the government, in effect, Why does this government allow itself to be an international outcast? That isn't good for the government of Burma, and it isn't good for companies like Unocal doing business with it. Unocal representatives have suggested some steps that the government could take to make matters better.

Further, company representatives have regularly spoken on behalf of political prisoners, including Aung San Suu Kyi. Now that Aung San Suu Kyi has been released, Unocal plans to continue to speak for her and others. In fact, Unocal has asked a professional human rights activist to advise them on further practical and systematic steps it can take on behalf of human rights. It monitors appeals for assistance to individuals, and tries to bring to bear quiet but effective help.

Since the company intends to have a long-term relation with Burma, it is convinced that it must forge good relations with all parts of the population. It does not wish to identify itself with the regime, or play a political role, or interfere in the nation's internal affairs. In fact, it cannot, under U.S. law.

Unocal's interests, its leaders point out, are in the long run more involved with the people of Burma than with any transient regime. In addition, it can and does perform services in the current strained circumstances that the government cannot. As Harvard professor Spar writes, "In the pursuit of making money, multinationals will—with some exceptions—tend to boost host-country economic development, raise labor standards, and possibly even loosen political restraints." Unocal has undertaken several human development initiatives—in hygiene, education, and environmental preservation—that would be beyond the capacities of the Burmese government. The interests of Unocal are larger than its connections with the government.

That Unocal must make human rights arguments, both to be true to its own identity as an American firm and to protect its name in its short-term as well as long-term interests, I am absolutely certain. A great deal of imagination and innovation is being expended on this task. One difficulty all such firms face, however, is that they cannot go public on everything they do. It is not proper (neither lawful nor practical) for them to become confrontational with the regime. To announce publicly everything they do, furthermore, would injure their effectiveness. Governments are proud and will do many things privately that they would resist if they were to be trumpeted in public.

Besides, deeds count more than words. Some in the "human rights community" (i.e., public advocates) respect this principle; a few prefer confrontation with the companies and demand in turn that the companies become confrontational with offending regimes. To the principle, "Deeds matter more than words," I would add, "Practical results matter more than rhetoric."

As in Unocal's case, a Western firm doing business with a dictatorship (or any other government) accrues diplomatic responsibilities of both a moral and political nature. The relationship is not, and cannot be construed as, a purely economic relationship. The world does not work that way. Like it or not, moral and political judgments about Unocal are being made by observers this very minute.

Of course, Unocal has not forgotten that its primary purpose is a limited economic task, which in itself will redound to the benefit of the people of Burma. Neither has it tried to evade being who it is, under the moral obligations that its own identity thrusts on it. It would not dream of pretending to be a company of automatons or moral ciphers; that would violate its entire corporate culture. It knows it needs to explore its moral possibilities imaginatively and to acquit all its duties to itself, its employees, its stockholders, and the system in which they participate. Unocal accepts this challenge openly and is not hesitant about defending its actions.

One further avenue open to Unocal is to seek the assistance of various outside human rights groups that are not reflexively anticapitalist, in order to consult on practical actions that are open to it and likely to be of good effect. In fact, Unocal has done this. What the result will be is not yet known. But the standards by which Unocal asks to be judged—its "Statement of Principles"—are high.

In sum, human rights cases are notoriously delicate and difficult. But how they are resolved is plainly of great significance for the future of this planet. Now that human rights abuses are likely to be found in smaller nations under the sway of dictators and outside the context of the cold war, companies can learn from one another's experiences, as they establish a new era in the interaction of companies with tyrants.

In China, for example, government officials demanded that

Pfizer, the pharmaceutical company, report back to it on the behavior of its Chinese employees. When Pfizer refused, the Chinese authorities dropped the matter. I would like to see Pfizer, Unocal, and other companies that can show successes in this field band together in their own human rights business coalition to strengthen one another's knowledge and effectiveness.

The calling of business is to support the reality and reputation of capitalism, democracy, and moral purpose everywhere, and not in any way to undermine them.

Chapter Nine

✧

MAKING THINGS BETTER

> Among laws controlling human societies there is one
> more precise and clearer, it seems to me, than all the oth-
> ers. If men are to remain civilized or to become civilized,
> the art of association must develop and improve among
> them at the same speed as equality of conditions
> spreads.
>
> —*Alexis de Tocqueville*

The dynamism driving a capitalist system forward, we have seen,
is the virtue of creative initiative. The other side of that virtue is
the responsibilities it imposes. Implicit in that dynamism is a
commitment to make things better. The assumption behind it is
that the Creator did not make the world finished but to be finished. His purpose in making women and men in his image was
to draw them into his own creative work as co-creators.

To be sure, humans are not creators in the same sense as God is; we do not make things out of nothing. If we had not first received, we would be unable to create in any sense. Given the unformed, evolving, and ever-changing world of nature and history and given the talents, abilities, and vocations endowed in us by the Creator—and only then because we have first received—we can lend ourselves to the Creator's service, so that he might act through us as he wills.

"Be it done to me according to thy will" is the fundamental form of prayer, work, and action of Jews, Christians, and Muslims. We open ourselves so that he might act through us.

This means, among other things, that we must always be looking around at the world in which we find ourselves, in order to discern ways in which God's will might be better done.

The world, as we find it, is full of faults and incompleteness. It constantly beckons us with more yet to be done, better ways to be found, faults and evils to be corrected.

Consider some examples.

THE BAD SIDE OF DOWNSIZING

In the early chapters of this book we encountered at least two examples of the anguish caused to managers by the necessity of letting good people go in order to save the firm.

In communist societies, dissidents and other "misfits" were often punished by being removed from their jobs. Sometimes they were sent to prison, sometimes placed in menial employment. My good friend Pavel Bratinka of the Czech Republic, now deputy foreign minister, was a distinguished young physicist until he joined the dissident movement Charter 77. He was summarily deprived of his opportunities for research and teaching and sentenced to working as a stoker in the coal-burning heating units of a large building. The current cardinal archbishop of Prague was sentenced to working as a window washer.

Nonetheless, practically everybody in communist societies was put to work. Even if much of this work was senseless—simply to meet production quotas piling up steel beams that nobody wanted to buy outside the plant in Nowa Huta, Poland, where they rusted away; bringing in fish from the cold Bering Sea to rot in broken refrigeration units—today some remember those days with nostalgia: "We were all equal and everybody had a job."

In a far more intelligent way, based on the dynamism of markets and invention, the German social market economy goes to extraordinary lengths to protect workers, once hired, from being laid off. It also provides very high benefits and expensive social plans for any who are let go. In protecting the security of the workforce, the German system (imitated in other European nations) has given democracy a stable popular base. Having experienced devastating periods of insecurity during World War I, the skyrocketing inflation of the 1920s, the Great Depression, and then World War II and its at first bleak aftermath, Germans tend to value security higher than most other social goods. They also tend to favor equality over opportunity. They prefer a stable society in which the incomes of all are more or less equal to a society in which there are more risks but chances for greater rewards. Even when assured that the incomes of all would be higher in the opportunity society but more unequal, they prefer equality at lower levels.

One disadvantage from which the German system suffers is that employers fear hiring new workers because of the high and lasting costs to which each employment contract commits them. Those currently employed are privileged; entry for others is difficult. Another disadvantage is that the German system sets many legal and financial hurdles before new entrepreneurs. The result is low rates of new business formation and high rates of unemployment.

A third disadvantage is that in the new international competition, German firms are more straitjacketed than their U.S. and Japanese counterparts. It is far harder for them to restructure themselves and redeploy their energies.

Fourth, as German women continue to have fewer children, the aging of the working population and the swelling ranks of the retired elderly are straining the finances of the welfare state. A similar situation in the United States is somewhat eased by the great influx of immigrants, most of whom become citizens. Since 1970, America has welcomed nearly 20 million legal immigrants (as well as many illegals). This immigration has increased the younger U.S. workforce by a number larger than the workforce of several medium-sized European nations put together.

Nonetheless, if it makes little sense for the United States to imitate German ways, we still need to improve the way in which assistance is offered to those laid off as a result of downsizing and restructuring. The situation of middle-aged and older workers is particularly affecting.

One important reform would be to vest health care plans in each worker, so that each plan will go wherever the individual goes. There is no reason, only historical accident, that companies should be the carriers of health care plans. In fact, much of the increase in workers' compensation packages in recent decades comes from increases in health care coverage—both to cover higher costs and to include new medical technologies. This is a major reason that the wages of many have grown only slowly; they are taking an ever larger proportion of their compensation in benefit packages, including enriched health care benefits. For example, the health care costs for all workers at General Motors in 1970 were $359 million, but by 1992 $3.7 billion. (In constant 1970 dollars, the jump was from $359 million to $1.03 billion.)

One reason for raising compensation by way of benefits rather than wages goes back to the wage and price controls introduced by the Nixon administration. Another is that benefits come to the worker tax free, and this fact appeals to workers. Receiving such benefits through the company, however, has had negative side effects: because workers are tied to the company as never before, to depart from the company means losing benefits. Lack of portability makes workers dependent.

High labor costs resulting from generous benefit packages also give companies an incentive to alter their approach to labor in unfortunate ways—by shedding many long-term jobs, for example. Large corporations began contracting out many services (security, maintenance and clean-up, food services, accounting, etc.) that were formerly supplied through the organization itself. Lack of stability in the labor force has badly affected morale, among white-collar workers as well as blue collar, and not least in middle management.

The tragedy of recent decades is that many senior workers, in higher as well as lower ranks, suffered a double disadvantage. First, their very jobs became vulnerable to cost-cutting and restructuring. Second, those whose jobs were terminated abruptly found themselves without basic benefits on which they and their families had come to rely, most notably health care protection and in many cases pension benefits.

To remedy this situation, another structural reform that has won considerable political support among both Democrats and Republicans is to make not only health care but also pensions portable. Instead of belonging to the company, such benefits would be owned by individual workers. Through programs such as TIAA-CREF, for example, most universities, colleges, and nonprofit organizations (such as museums, research institutes, and foundations) provide pension plans that insure a multitude of institutions while granting ownership in the benefits to each individual worker, and allowing each to choose (up to certain limits) certain options for themselves: how much additional money to save tax-free in their personal accounts; in which investment vehicle to invest it; and how they wish to receive the benefits when they become eligible for them. Such workers carry these benefits with them from job to job.

In general, individual retirement accounts (IRAs) heighten a sense of individual responsibility, independence, and mobility. Since such savings are tax-free, they also provide powerful incentives for lifetime investment.

Analogously, well short of the ill-fated "comprehensive" health care plan proposed by the Clinton administration, considerable consensus exists on *incremental* health care reforms, medical IRAs, for example.

Forbes magazine has pioneered an intermediate arrangement. While offering its employees a form of catastrophic medical insurance, insuring them against unexpectedly high medical costs, the company also offers a package covering ordinary medical claims but with a twist. The entire package of ordinary health care is worth $1,500 per year, but individuals are offered an incentive to keep actual costs lower. For every dollar in their personal medical account that they choose *not* to spend in that year, up to $500, *Forbes* will double that amount in a cash payment to that individual. In other words, for every dollar that individuals save (up to $500) of their own medical bills or simply do not withdraw from their individual annual account, they will be paid an equal amount in cash. This plan gives employees a financial incentive to keep a close watch on their out-of-pocket health expenses, to make their own medical decisions, and to keep group costs low. Each year since the plan was instituted in 1992, employees have received greater cash benefits, and medical costs to *Forbes* have fallen. Individual responsibility—and satisfaction—have been enhanced.

One of the disadvantages of the "creative destruction" inherent in a system based on invention, creativity, and new methods, in short, is the insecurity of employees. Creative thinking about how to diminish this insecurity is very much in

order. The personal ownership of benefit packages, particularly
for pension and health care benefits, and their portability from
job to job, are two powerful steps in the right direction.

NEW IDEAS FOR LABOR UNIONS

Trying to peer ahead into the future, we see a world in which
industries will frequently be trying to reinvent themselves in
order to meet changing demand in the marketplace and new
technological possibilities. The flexibility of the labor force will
become a great competitive advantage of some nations over
others. What can labor unions do to help?

In such circumstances, it may be possible for some labor
unions, at least on local or regional levels, to organize themselves as independent business corporations, supplying trained
and intelligent workers, as needed, to other corporations.
Consider communications workers. Instead of merely organizing the communications workers currently employed by a local
telephone company and other similar organizations, and bargaining company by company for new contracts for their workers, why not try a new approach? Beginning incrementally, the
communications workers of a certain area (say, Communications Workers of Miami, Inc.) might incorporate themselves as
a service corporation offering a body of trained workers with the
widest possible range of specialties and skills, seeking individu-
ally tailored contracts with employers of all kinds. These contracts could run for various lengths of time and special circumstances. These workers would have the union as their primary employer; their secondary employer would be the company with which the new contract is written. Such workers
could be hired at premium wages and still save their secondary
employers significant sums, since their employment would be
on a limited time basis. Meanwhile, every worker of CWM, Inc.,
would own stock in CWM, Inc., which in turn would be capi-

talized as an employee stock ownership partnership (ESOP). The fate of the workers would no longer be tied to the vicissitudes of any one company in the region, as it now is, but to the entire market for communications workers.

This approach has some untraditional assumptions. During the early industrial age, we all became accustomed to thinking of a job as a kind of lifetime contract. Technological changes were for a long time few, and entire industries grew accustomed to long time frames and more or less fixed processes and methods. Looking into the future, however, we see that international competition in new technologies and methods requires that entire industries keep on top of rapidly changing markets worldwide. Italy's Rocco Buttiglione warns Italian voters that there will be new multitudes of "work opportunities," but fewer permanent, lifetime "jobs." Nations will always need a strong and highly skilled labor force, with workers who are flexible, adaptive, and equal to rapidly changing market demands. Leading countries will have to multiply work opportunities for their labor force, without enjoying the earlier luxury of offering many lifetime jobs.

Given the needs of a rapidly changing world, in which more and more peoples begin the ascent out of poverty and become active participants in worldwide markets, there is bound to be an abundance of work opportunities. But many of these opportunities will not be of limitless duration; rather, ever new restructurings will impose upon them kaleidoscopic change.

Labor unions, formed in the crucible of long, slow industrial change, will do well to get out in front of the new electronic era. By restructuring themselves as service corporations offering skilled, adaptive labor forces to rapidly changing industries, they might become crucial new players in the world of always shifting work opportunities. Their power at the bargaining table would be much enhanced. The job security of their workers would be secured in a new way. The workers would gain in independence from any one contracting company. The competitive advantage they would offer is know-how and creative adaptation.

It is probably unreasonable to expect that all unions should or could restructure themselves in this way. But though the idea may seem paradoxical, some could consider this crucial fact: one of the greatest sources of wealth creation and value-added is a highly skilled, creative, and flexible workforce. Unions might well become owners and managers of this great source of wealth, seeking ever fresh contracts for its fruitful and happy employment.

ORGANIZING TO HELP THE HOMELESS

The great story line of the twentieth century has been the promise that the centralized, administrative state could guarantee security, health, and welfare to all its citizens. The dream of the national collective inspired intellectuals and avant-garde dreamers almost everywhere, and for a time, this dream bore fruit. Partly under the impulse of the great wars that marked the twentieth century, immense centralization was achieved, of an intrusiveness and power never before imagined. Yet at a certain point it began to be obvious to most that this emperor wore no clothes. The state turned out to be, increasingly, the great overpromiser and underachiever of our time. Supporting its ambitious programs became an impossible tax burden, and it paid for its good results in some fields by rapid social decline in others. The state, it turned out, is a morally dubious master.

One casualty of the welfare state in advanced societies is the national budget; the welfare state has made financial promises that it can no longer keep. A more serious casualty is the growing dependency of people on government and a correlative decline in important virtues. Welfare benefits have corrupted the daily truth telling of entire professions—for example, through physicians' signing forms documenting "disabilities" for which benefits are available, in such numbers as are hardly to be believed. The most serious casualty of all is the decline of the family. The proportion of children born out of wedlock in Germany is now 15 percent, in Britain 33 percent, in the United States 30 percent, and in Sweden almost twice as high as in the United States (although in Sweden many couples live in long-term cohabitation, without benefit of marriage).

Along with the decline of strong and virtue-teaching families is a relatively new curse: the widespread use of mind-damaging drugs, alcohol abuse, and other self-destructive forms of social conduct. In the United States, a significant proportion of such social damage shows up among the homeless, many of whom need medical treatment at least as much as they need homes. Indeed, many of the homeless actually have homes or at least family members with whom they often stay, but not always. For certain periods, spasmodically, many of them turn to living on the streets. Whatever the reasons or the circumstances, they need care, even if they themselves sometimes resist obtaining it.

At the same time as many Americans and others are recognizing that solving many social problems is beyond the capacity of the administrative state—indeed, that many new social problems seem to arise *from* the practices of the welfare state—they are turning for remedies to the institutions of civil society. In practice, this means turning to self-governing citizens—to *us*—to find realistic solutions outside government.

With regard to the homeless particularly, skillful and practical leaders of the business community, both large businesses and small, should take dramatic steps in the name of self-government to remedy this social need. Consider an analogous problem: feeding the hungry. In some cities, business coalitions against hunger have already been formed. Virtually all large food stores end each day with foodstuffs they remove from their shelves, still edible and useful; the same is true with hotels and restaurants. Rather than throwing this food away, business coalitions have arranged for trucks to pick up donated food and bring it to a collection center, from which it is then distributed to food shelters and other helping agencies for the benefit of the needy. Organizational skill is necessary, as are volunteer labor, part-time donation of trucks and other transport, and a modest outlay of funds. Invited to participate, citizens are quite willing and able to practice such works of social justice and love, for the good of the city.

Similar results might be achieved by farsighted civic leaders committed to organizing members of the legal and medical professions, builders, realtors, fund raisers, and others to meet the basic needs of the homeless, seen on the streets of most cities today. Nearly all the homeless need medical examinations and basic medical care; many need counseling; some are demonstrably unable to take responsibility for their own care. In most localities, ordinances of law need to be changed if better care is to be provided. Those in need of medical help may be unwilling to seek it themselves. For such reasons, lawyers and judges may need to be brought into the coalition. Religious leaders and educators, not to mention the editors of local media, may contribute other practical ideas.

Community by community, the dimensions of the problem are not so great that they defy solution—or at least significant amelioration. Such efforts on behalf of the common good are more safely undertaken by the institutions of civil society, including business as a primary source of leadership, than by the state.

SOLIDARITY WITH THE WORLD'S POOR

Alfred Whittaker was made president of Bristol-Myers International Corp. just as his children were leaving the nest, and one of the perks offered him by the company, to compensate him for the heavy travel schedule the job entailed, was the opportunity to take his wife, Marion, with him on his business trips. The couple built a new house on five acres in the New Jersey countryside. They were enjoying the prestige, high salary, first-class travel, breathtaking sightseeing, and the job itself, when suddenly President Whittaker was stricken by—a sermon.

One Sunday, just over a year after Whittaker had taken on the new job in 1971, with all its rewards and perks, he and Marion heard a sermon at a Bible conference near their home. The pastor didn't understand much about business, but he did outline the need for an organization that would help the poor in developing nations to create jobs. This passage in the sermon lasted only a minute, but it hit Whittaker forcefully. When he spoke to his wife afterward, she had already formed the same decision.

A few months later, Whittaker had quit his job, exchanged his plush corporate office for a low-rent tiny one with a single metal desk, sold the big house, and began organizing Opportunity International (OI), a nonprofit organization whose purpose is to teach the chronically poor of the third world how to start, run, and develop small businesses, in order to make the new entrepreneurs self-sufficient and able to provide goods, services, and jobs to others.

Opportunity International does not give money to anyone. Rather, it sets up a local board of directors in every country in which it operates. This board identifies promising entrepreneurs to whom it lends money and offers advice, oversight, and technical education. OI finds it more efficient and trustworthy to obtain cooperation from local church people, who know the reliable entrepreneurs in their midst, and receive great satisfaction from seeing local conditions improve. The idea is to get the projects to succeed (in part, so as to have the borrowed money repaid, but even more as a measure of self-sufficiency achieved).

On his travels, Whittaker had noted how eager many of the world's poor are to better the condition of their families and how hard they are willing to work. But they lack two crucial ele-

ments of success: training in the simple know-how of successful business and a place to raise capital (outside the exorbi-
tantly usurious black market). Most of the loans made by OI
fall between the local equivalent of $25 and $800. Shoemakers,
fruit stand operators, truckers who take a village's produce to
the city, clothing makers, flower growers, local bakers: all such
small businesses can be put into operation with a relatively
small investment, provided there is a simple but solid business
plan underneath them.

A baker, for example, who needs the initial investment for
an oven and a few materials, can sell bread and cakes every day
and plough the money back into fresh materials, setting aside a
little every day for repaying the loan. Once it is repaid, she (I
am thinking of just such a woman in São Paolo, Brazil, in the
favela of St. Francis of Assisi) may come back for another loan,
to buy a larger oven. Her neighbors buy food previously not
available (she also keeps a big pot of hot cereal on the stove for
feeding children), and as her profits expand, she hires more
help and prepares more food than before. The people in all the
alleys around her shop benefit. Other entrepreneurs in her
favela are opening other businesses: several of the men are
bringing electric wires to shanty after shanty, one at a time.

In 1994, OI gave out more than 24,000 loans, worth about
$12 million, and generated about 64,000 jobs—humble jobs,
to be sure, but perhaps as meaningful as any jobs ever created.
When one meal a day rises to three meals a day for a family, or
when a cardboard/plywood roof is replaced by a metal roof, or
polluted water by potable water, or thin flat cakes by good
fresh bread, life has significantly improved. There is no reason
such grassroots progress cannot continue, slowly and steadily,
with each passing decade. At a certain point, progress is fed by
progress, and just as there have been vicious circles in the past,
beneficent circles can also gather force.

The loan repayment rate for OI hovers between 93 and 97
percent, a fabulous rate.

It has long been my own dream that every multinational corporation in the world would recruit volunteers from among its own retirees or members of its workforce families to give a year or so of their lives to help train and advise eager entrepreneurs in countries where the company does business. Even if they adopted just one *barrio* or *favela* every five years and then moved on to another, they could do many modest things that would have great effect. Donations from throughout the corporation could be solicited for lending programs like that of OI.

Maybe a few nurses could train some local people in first aid and basic care. Maybe a few teachers could volunteer to set up small lending libraries. Carpenters, bricklayers, and electricians could be extremely helpful in these struggling areas.

Of course, most companies are already having an impact simply by investing in poor countries, bringing in capital and technology otherwise not available, training workers for a wide range of tasks (from company lunch rooms to cleaning crews, as well as in business tasks). Often they build infirmaries and schools, put in roads and electric power lines, and in other ways contribute to building up the local infrastructure.

Yet there is no substitute for a more direct and hands-on set of programs to help the poor. Companies have only scratched the surface in turning their imaginations and creative and organizational talents to changing the fate of the poor in the countries in which they do business.

A friend of mine sent to Africa by a major U.S. softdrink firm some decades ago saw to it—he had the discretion to act as he saw fit—that as many black Africans were set up in business as he could manage, in all the satellite tasks necessary for building a bottling plant and transport system. Every such plant generates supporting businesses, from window cleaners to truckers, from pipefitters to lunch room workers. He argued that it would be a great local advantage to his company to have in place a sound history of rooting itself among indigenous people. And so it now has.

Chapter Ten

✣

GIVING IT ALL AWAY

It is clear that when people make the effort, not only are causes and other people helped, but something very special happens to the giver too, and in the combination, the community and the nation take on a spirit of compassion, comradeship, and confidence.

—Brian O'Connell

When he was only thirty-three years old, in 1868, Andrew Carnegie wrote out a note to himself that must have made him uneasy for many years thereafter. It began in a complacent tone: "Thirty three and an income of 50,000$ per annum. By this time two years I can so arrange all my business as to secure at least 50,000 per annum." But Carnegie did not think that business alone was his calling.

At thirty-three, he dreamed of a future career spent in literary circles. At the end of two years, he commanded himself, "Cast aside business forever except for others." After that, "Settle in Oxford & get a thorough education making the acquaintance of literary men—this will take three years of active work—pay especial attention to speaking in public." But the most significant words he wrote that cold December day in the St. Nicholas Hotel were these:

> Man must have an idol—The amassing of wealth is one of the worst species of idolitary [*sic*]. No idol more debasing than the worship of money. Whatever I engage in I must push inordinately therefor should I be careful to choose that life which will be the most elevating in its character. To continue much longer overwhelmed by business cares and with most of my thoughts wholly upon the way to make more money in the shortest time, must degrade me beyond hope of permanent recovery.

Carnegie did not in fact stop creating new industries and new technologies in 1870, as he here promised. But he did stop in 1901 and spent the rest of his life—some seventeen years—giving all of his money away. He did this according to a scheme he devised in his most famous article, which appeared first in the United States in June and December 1889 and the following year in Britain. When it first appeared in the preeminent literary magazine, the *North American Review*, its title was, as Carnegie had given it, "Wealth," but the editors who published it in Britain gave it the somewhat misleading title by which it subsequently became known worldwide: "The Gospel of Wealth." The British title suggested that the getting of wealth was Carnegie's gospel—a false gospel. To the contrary, Carnegie's explicit point was the opposite: while the amassing of wealth by a few is inevitable, the true gospel is giving it away—and giving it away in a manner that helps the poor.

To a remarkable degree, a consistent thread in Carnegie's

complicated moral life was his desire to help the poor. In the St. Nicholas memorandum, for example, he outlined what he would do after his three years at Oxford (just enough, by the way, for the standard Oxford undergraduate education):

> Settle then in London & purchase a controlling interest in some newspaper or live review & give the general management of it attention [Carnegie's special gift], taking a part in public matters especially those concerned with education & improvement of the poorer classes.

Carnegie never forgot what growing up poor was like. He never forgot what not having a chance to complete more than four years of education was like. He felt himself all his life running breathless to catch up. Even at the age of thirty-three, he concluded the memo with the pledge that before he resigned from business forever, at thirty-five, during the ensuing two years, he would "spend the afternoons in securing instruction, and in reading systematically."

Morally, Carnegie was a far more interesting man than one consumed by greed. It will be satisfying one day to know how a good and merciful God welcomed him for his final accounting and weighed his trespasses.

Religiously, Carnegie appears to have been thoroughly secular. He was the only child in his neighborhood allowed to spend Sunday mornings skating on the ice of the neighboring Allegheny River, while the others were in church. He seemed tone-deaf regarding God. While it is true that one of his favorite charities was the gift of pipe organs to churches around the world (7,689 in total), he antagonized scores of local ministers regularly and seemed to relish doing so. Possibly, his fear of falling down before an idol arose because he was deaf to God. Fearing God's judgment, he would have had no need to fear the attraction of any worldly idol.

Yet how does a man tell whether he loves God? No one sees God, St. John reminds us in his First Letter (4:12): "No man has ever seen God; but if we love one another, then we have God dwelling in us. . . . This is our proof that we are dwelling in Him, and He in us."

Moreover, Carnegie failed to make the crucial distinction between making money and creating new wealth. Carnegie did not just make money. He created new models of large-scale management, new technologies, a new industry, scores of thousands of new jobs, and entirely new possibilities for human civilization significant enough to generate an era of human history named the Age of Steel. Had he kept his promise of 1868, before his great accomplishments in the field of industry had gotten underway, the world today would be a poorer place. Within a capitalist system, great pioneers and inventors are not trapped in a zero-sum game, in which what one wins, others lose. What creators gain, they are not taking from others. They create vast amounts of wholly new wealth from which all of society benefits, of which what they receive through stock ownership is only a small fraction. The genius deployed throughout the Carnegie Corporation bettered life for billions of persons through new uses opened up for steel, from girders for skyscrapers to tableware, from rust-free and wear-ever train rails (replacing rapidly worn iron) to lightweight sheet metal for the sides of automobiles.

Carnegie did not keep his promise of 1868 in 1870—did not keep it until 1901. He is one of the rare wealthy men in history who early on decided that the point of life is to give away his wealth. You can't take it with you. He gave decades of thought to how best to give wealth away, especially for the benefit of the poor.

In facing that question ourselves, it's worth beginning with Andrew Carnegie's stimulating proposals. Not many others have left behind such detailed advice.

CARNEGIE'S STRATEGY

"There are but three modes in which surplus wealth can be disposed of," Carnegie reflected. "It can be left to the families of the decedents; or it can be bequeathed for public purposes; or, finally, it can be administered by its possessors during their lives."

As for the first of these, observation led Carnegie to say that in most cases a large legacy is a disaster for those on the receiving end. Large legacies tend to breed dependency, weakness, and uncreative lives. Seldom does one find "millionaires' sons unspoiled by wealth, who, being rich, still perform great services to the community. Such are the very salt of the earth, as valuable as, unfortunately, they are rare." Those planning their own estates must expect the general rule to apply, not the exception. "I would as soon leave to my son a curse as the almighty dollar," a thoughtful man must say, Carnegie concluded. If you think of the welfare of the children rather than family pride, you are not likely to leave much of your wealth to them.

Regarding the second option, bequeathing one's wealth for public purposes, Carnegie observes that "knowledge of the results of legacies bequeathed is not calculated to inspire the brightest hopes of much posthumous good being accomplished by them. The cases are not few in which the real object sought by the testator is not attained, nor are they few in which his real wishes are thwarted. In many cases the bequests are so used as to become only monuments of his folly."

Only the third option seemed fitting to Carnegie. Rich persons blessed with management talents, vision, and imagination ought to make an art of giving their fortunes away. If they have known what it is to be poor, they will know from experience what helps the poor to rise above poverty. The duty of the person of wealth, Carnegie wrote, is to live modestly and without ostentation, and to consider all surplus revenues which come to him simply as trust funds, which he is called upon to administer, and strictly bound as matter of duty to administer in the manner which, in his judgment, is best calculated to produce the most beneficial results for the community—the man of wealth thus becoming the mere trustee and agent for his poorer brethren.

Having been poor, Carnegie had seen how charity works from the bottom up. He was opposed to "relief," almsgiving, small amounts spread broadly without clear knowledge of how they would be spent. "Of every one thousand dollars spent in so-called charity today, it is probable that nine hundred and fifty dollars is unwisely spent—so spent, indeed, as to produce the very evils which it hopes to mitigate or cure."

Carnegie was most deeply impressed by the great good done, generation after generation, by the money Peter Cooper had invested in the Cooper Institute, by the "five millions given by Mr. Tilden for a free library in the city of New York," by the establishment of Stanford University by the Stanford family, and by the gifts of Enoch Pratt of Baltimore, Charles Pratt of Brooklyn, and others. Of those who die with available wealth not yet well put to public benefit, Carnegie wrote: "The man who dies thus rich dies disgraced."

There was certainly paternalism in Carnegie's views. He knew from experience that he could administer a great corporation—bigger than any before envisioned—with skills that few others possessed. He knew his own gifts. This led him to think that such gifts ought to be put to the service of philanthropy, too, not just business. He did not mind thinking that he could put wealth to use for the poor better than the poor could put it to use for themselves. That is how he had created jobs that they could not create for themselves. Besides, when he had been poor, Colonel James Anderson of Allegheny, who provided him and his friends with access to his private collection of four hundred books, had done more to change their lives than any other benefaction they had experienced or observed.

There was also a touch of the grandiose in Carnegie's views. He thought his views would be an effective answer to communism, as if they represented a full-dress system. In his own approach, however, it is obvious that Carnegie concentrated only on some of the poor, "the industrious and ambitious; not those who need everything done for them, but those who, being most anxious and able to help themselves, deserve and will be benefitted by help from others and by the extension of their opportunities."

Carnegie thought city or state could provide "refuge" for those lacking the drive to improve their own condition—feed, clothe, shelter them—and at best thought philanthropy might try to inspire them, elevate their sights, and refresh their spirits by certain public works.

Without comment, let us now list the seven "best uses" for wealth that Carnegie had by 1888 winnowed out from everything he had seen.

First, standing apart by itself is the founding of a university. . . .

Second, a free library, provided a community will accept and maintain it as a public institution, as much so as its public schools. . . .

Third, the founding or extension of hospitals, medical colleges, laboratories, and other institutions connected with the alleviation of human suffering, and especially with the prevention rather than with the cure of human ills.

Fourth, public parks, always provided that the community undertakes to maintain, beautify, and preserve them inviolate; and conservatories.

Fifth, for our cities, halls suitable for meetings of all kinds, as well as concert and opera halls.

Sixth, swimming pools for people, as in Europe.

Seventh, churches are not exactly public benefactions [Carnegie jabbed ministers again] but sectarian, best left to the individual consciences of donors; but some churches do serve as public meeting houses, especially in certain districts, and these make worthy objects of philanthropy.

It is open to everybody, of course, to make up other lists of priorities. Some items on this list may have made more sense in 1888 than they do today, a hundred years later. Some items lead us to be grateful that great philanthropists so well met such goals generations ago: the parks, the conservatories, the music halls that we have so much enjoyed and (often) taken for granted.

Andrew Carnegie and John D. Rockefeller are usually credited with pioneering the path of the giant givers of modern philanthropy. For some years, the world's newspapers kept score on the giving. The *London Times* reported that in 1903 Carnegie had given away $21 million, Rockefeller $10 million. By 1910, the *New York American*'s box score (for lifetime giving) read: Rockefeller $134,271,000, Carnegie an even grander $179,300,000. All this was before the income tax and other tax provisions had generated external incentives to giving. The feeling of duty to the public good arose from inner sources. By 1913, the *New York Herald* ran a final box score: "Carnegie, $332 million; Rockefeller, $175 million."

By this time, Carnegie had been defeated in his pledge to give all his wealth away under his own direction. The task was simply too fatiguing, too overwhelming, and (since he could never give money away fast enough), too disheartening. Each project took some study, and scores of thousands of requests poured in. By the time he had, through his own decisions, given away $180 million, his fortune had grown through the magic of compound interest to a sum nearly as large as when he started. The faster he ran, the further out of reach his goal seemed. His biographer quotes him as saying as an aside to a speech in those days: "Millionaires who laugh are rare, very rare, indeed."

Resigned to his fate, Carnegie transmitted nearly all that remained to the largest philanthropic trust ever before known, the Carnegie Corporation. No man can know everything and do everything; he had run headlong into his own finitude.

Alas, Carnegie then gave his trust only vague stipulations for its use, entrusting decisions to the judgment of future trustees. His earlier observations about how he had seen such bequests turned against the founder's wishes may have made him despair of trying to guide the programs of the future by written ordinances. Even more so today than in Carnegie's day, since our public consensus is less broad and deep, it is exceedingly difficult for a donor to be sure that future trustees will share his or her own moral and intellectual commitments or that recipients will use funds for the purposes (and in the spirit) intended in a founding grant. Even the most carefully written stipulation of purpose is quite often forgotten or, worse, rationalized away. This is especially true when the ideals of the donor—usually a man or woman whose wealth was earned through business—are privately scorned by those who actually get the money in their hands.

Carnegie had seen this happen to others. He hadn't wanted to be in this position but now felt he had no choice but to surrender. He may (or may not) have approved of the later decisions made by the trustees of his foundation. The sad point for him was that he abandoned his own basic principle: that the donor's own wisdom and experience ought to direct his philanthropy.

With the last great donation to the trust and a few others, Carnegie in the end gave away 90 percent of his fortune. Of the donations, 80 percent went to support the human mind: to universities, institutes, schools, libraries, grants and pensions for college teachers, and the like. On his own, he had been a patron of the work of Booker T. Washington, such "Negro" schools (as they were then called) as Tuskegee Institute and the Hampton

Institute, and those open to poor whites and blacks alike such as Berea College—usually choosing not to help the larger and more famous universities but seeking out smaller and strategically important ones. Now his fortune was in other hands.

IN GIVING, BE VIGILANT: CAVEAT DONOR!

If we think back to the autumn of 1945 when the ashes of World War II had barely ceased smoking in Germany and Japan, and when even Americans seem to have been—from a perspective fifty years later—so simple and poor a people, having raced from the Great Depression headlong into mass mobilization and sacrifice for the war effort, we may get some glimpse of the enormous growth of wealth in the world during the past fifty years. Think solely of the new technologies—and entirely new industries—that have come into existence during this period: in chemistry, metals, jet engines, radar, electronics, fiber optics, genetic medicines, copying machines, fax machines, cellular phones, satellite communications, and others. Perhaps never before has the wealth of the world increased so dramatically. In constant 1982 dollars, the gross national product of the United States jumped from $1.2 trillion in 1950 to $4.2 trillion in 1990. Then between January and September of 1995 alone, the value of all equity stocks on the U.S. stock exchanges increased by $1 trillion.

Something interesting is rumbling underneath this vast multiplication of wealth since 1945. Most of the creators of this new wealth who were young in the 1950s have begun making their wills, bequests, and trusts. From them and their immediate successors, between $20 and $30 trillion are expected to pour into philanthropy in the next thirty years, as the wealth creators of the recent era go home to the Lord. As Phil Merrill, publisher of the *Washingtonian*, has said, Don't think only of the Warren Buffetts and Bill Gates of the world but also of the less well-known, local, almost invisible small fortunes in every city of the nation.

Think of the new buildings that have gone up around the center of Washington in an ever-expanding ring since 1960, Merrill notes. All of those buildings have owners. Each represents a small fortune. Home values, too, have increased, by 1,000 percent since 1945. One of the greatest transfers of private wealth in history is going to take place during the next thirty years, and a great proportion of it will go to philanthropy. Where else can that wealth go? Perhaps more important, where else would most American families want it to go, tax deductions or not?

People in business tend to justify the amounts they give in terms of tax deductions, Merrill says, but most of them give because they want to. That's what Americans do. Most have known some poverty, and they want to "pay back." They are thankful, and want to express their gratitude in real terms. They want to strengthen the system they love.

Like Carnegie, many want to support education, research, and other works of the mind. As we have seen, that is exactly how new wealth is generated. Many of them also understand that since the 1960s, the culture of the universities and colleges has separated itself to a remarkable degree from mainstream culture, especially from business culture. In the real world, socialism may have died an ugly death, but on campuses, where whole careers have been based on anticapitalist premises, change is not so sudden. Some academic preferences face few real-world tests. Many of the courses in multiculturalism, race, and gender—and campus-wide emphases on "diversity"— have anticapitalism as a main pillar of their agenda.

For those persons of wealth, great or modest, who wish to endow programs defending the virtues and main ideas of the Western tradition, in order to carry forward into another generation the spiritual and intellectual resources that proved invaluable to them, great frustrations often lie in wait. Influential academic elites, especially in the humanities and social sciences, treat both American culture in particular and Western culture in general as enemies that need to be overthrown. They are often hostile to Judaism and Christianity, as religions that do not treat homosexuality as morally equivalent to the love of man and wife and that for the most part speak of God in masculine imagery. The good news is that they tend to favor democracy, although often in a utopian French way rather than in the tradition of Anglo-American realism. The bad news is that they tend to show disdain for the necessary condition of democracy: capitalism, and cognate realities such as commerce, entrepreneurship, private property, profits, and markets. Actual socialists in America are few, but academic anticapitalists are many—and not just critics of "abuses," as most businesspeople are too, but anticapitalists who see the moral structure of the system dimly, if at all.

From all this, only one general caution is possible: Donor beware! *Caveat donor!*

One crucial problem in launching a private foundation is that the sort of person drawn to working there does not as a rule share the worldview and experiences that grow out of a life in business. In less than a generation, private foundations are usually completely captured by a new point of view—sometimes on the part of trustees, often on the part of staff. Foundations of this type frequently go in directions opposite to the most cherished purposes and values of the donor. Paraphrasing Yogi Berra, "If the original donors were still alive, they'd be turning over in their graves." The MacArthur Foundation is a classic example of an institution founded by a very conservative donor turned in an extreme leftward direction.

Thus, some donors have written into their trusts a self-liquidating clause, figuring that the best they can do is make it probable that their trust will remain faithful to their purposes for twenty years. By then, all moneys must be expended. New York's Olin Foundation, for example, has chosen this route.

Giving money away is a refined art. Much intelligence and hard work has gone into earning it; sometimes even more is required to spend it wisely. To shovel it out the door is easy; to produce the desired effects and to choose the right hands to put it in are two far more difficult tasks.

This is not the place to present a primer on giving. Based on my own two years as a foundation officer at the Rockefeller Foundation (for over eighty years, one of the best of all foundations) and on observation since, I offer seven maxims:

1. The most important point is to identify the right person to work with at the receiving institution—someone who understands the grant's purposes clearly and has shown a life commitment in that direction.

2. If you want to give to an established institution, don't rely on its reputation. Get some help to research it and its leading persons thoroughly, even if your aim is general support of its long-term activities—and even more so if your aim is to contribute some new initiative. Money cannot buy a human will determined to do otherwise; it can only support a will already moved by its own love for the new initiative.

3. If you want to help a new or less well-known institution upgrade itself, be sure that the grant recipient truly welcomes outside assistance (all the way down the staff list), and be careful to identify two sets of outside persons: those who will be willing to join the receiving institution to help it move forward *and* who can work with the existing staff; and those who will be willing to serve on an outside advisory board for the project.

4. If you want to promote the pursuit of certain ideas or

the objective study of all the implications of certain ideas, policies, movements, or the like, it is probably best to establish an independent study center or think tank inside or outside the university setting, but in any case apart from the flow of ordinary university politics; *independent* is the key word.

5. It is probably wise to establish two sets of controls over your gift, even if (perhaps especially if) it is to a university: first, an outside advisory board to evaluate whether the grant is meeting the agreed-upon purposes established by the donor and welcomed by the receiving institution, meeting at least annually; and, second, to establish a time line so that if the grant is not meeting its purposes, it can be terminated after three years or five years.

6. Find the right environment for the right people. The "right" people need to be in tune with the grant's purposes, creative in their own right, competent in organization and administration, and skilled in working with colleagues—even hostile colleagues—in the larger institutional setting. But even the right people are helpless without suitable support in their institutional environment. Check this out carefully. Cynicism in the institution from above or below can undermine success even before it starts.

7. As Andrew Carnegie found, another condition is finding recipients who are willing to commit long-term institutional support of their own, as a warrant for their commitment to the grant's purposes. Absent this commitment, giving a grant is like spitting into the wind.

In brief, giving money wisely requires entirely new sets of concerns and skills. Don't be surprised by that. Most people—never having been rich before—just haven't thought about it.

THE GLORY OF THE NATION

What comes through from all of the great citizen movements of our history is that the participation, the caring, and the evidence that people can make a difference add wonderfully to the spirit of our society. Inez Haynes Irwin, in *The Story of Alice Paul*, repeatedly refers to the *spirit* of those women, not only in deciding on the task and accomplishing it, but in what their success meant to them as human beings. "They developed a sense of devotion to their ideal of freedom which would have stopped short of no personal sacrifice, not death itself. They developed a sense of comradeship for each other which was half love, half admiration and all reverence. In summing up a fellow worker, they speak first of her spirit, and her spirit is always *beautiful*, or *noble* or *glorious*."[9]

—*Brian O'Connell*

It is one of the greatest blessings of the United States to have in place so powerful a philanthropic tradition. Other democracies, notably Great Britain, have similar but somewhat less strong traditions. Independent of the state, many people now have many sources of capital to draw on for a multitude of projects in the realm of civil society—that is, in the realm of all those projects of self-government that citizens conceive of for themselves to strengthen public life. Few citizens anywhere desire to be wholly dependent on the state. The richly diverse vitalities of civil society spring from the benefactions of those who want to "give something back" to the principle of self-government that is the glory of free nations.

These multiple sources of private imagination and creativity, as active in the field of philanthropy as in the fields of commerce and industry, have already inspired some of the world's most beautiful architecture, splendid museums, spacious parks, excellent orchestras and ballet troupes, leading medical and other research centers, educational institutions, and even unusually successful programs for the poor.

Take away the world's private endowments and we would have a far less exciting—and less beautiful—civic landscape. In America, we have never had an aristocracy, and we have no feudal monuments, yet from the ranks of the financially successful, who were often born poor, stunning public benefactors have stepped forward. They have established one of the nation's best claims to originality among the nations. In this country the successful give generously to public purposes, with all the variety of individual imagination and all the vitality of a self-governing people.

Philanthropy is the mother's milk of civil society. Without needing to turn to government, here people turn to one another and accomplish public purposes.

Those whose calling is business do well to recognize early that, more than they may at first recognize, this calling leads to giving—and to the need to learn yet another civilizing art, the art of giving wisely.

Endnotes

✦

Author's note: Where sources are not indicated, I have drawn on personal correspondence and interviews conducted during 1994–1995.

Introduction

P. 1: Wolfe writes of "a stone, a leaf, an unfound door; of a stone, a leaf, a door. And of all the forgotten faces. . . . Which of us is not forever a stranger and alone? Remembering speechlessly we seek the great forgotten language, the lost lane-end into heaven, a stone, a leaf, an unfound door." *Look Homeward, Angel*, p. 1.

P. 2: Jacques Maritain writes on "knowledge by connaturality" in *The Range of Reason*, pp. 22–29, and many other works.

P. 6: Maritain discusses the influence of affluence on the human spirit at length in *Reflections on America*, particularly chapter IV, "The Old Tag of American Materialism," and chapter XVIII, "Work and Leisure."

P. 7: Michael Medved, *Hollywood vs. America*, pp. 220–222.

Pp. 8–9: On Bennett and Tucker's battle against Time Warner, see "Operation Time Warner" in *The American Enterprise*, July/August, 1995, pp. 8–9.

P. 13: Creative destruction is described by Schumpeter as a process "that incessantly revolutionizes the economic structure *from within*, incessantly destroying the old one, incessantly creating a new one. This process of Creative Destruction is the essential fact about capitalism. It is what capitalism consists in and what every capitalist concern has got to live in." *Capitalism, Socialism and Democracy*, p. 83.

Max Weber's essays "Politics as a Vocation" and "Science as a Vocation" can be found in *From Max Weber: Essays in Sociology*, translated by H. H. Gerth and C. Wright Mills, pp. 77–156.

Chapter One
WHAT IS A CALLING?

P. 17: Max Weber's idea of calling is drawn from *The Protestant Ethic and the Spirit of Capitalism*, p. 79.

P. 19: The anecdote concerning Peter can be found in M. Scott Peck, *A World Waiting to Be Born: Civility Rediscovered*, p. 222.

Pp. 20–21: Sir John Templeton is profiled by Lawrence Minard, *Forbes*, (January 16, 1995), pp. 67–74.

P. 23: On Lorraine Miller, see "Profits in Bloom," by Michael Barrier, *Nation's Business* (October 1995): 14. The same issue lists ten women who have founded important firms: Estée Lauder, cosmetics, 1946; Lillian Vernon, mail order, New York, 1951; Marian Ilitch, Little Caesar Enterprises, pizza chain, 1959; Frieda Caplan, Frieda's Finest Produce Specialties, wholesaler, 1962; Mary Kay Ash, Mary Kay Cosmetics, 1963; Ruth Fertel, Ruth's Chris Steak House, a national restaurant chain, 1965; Priscilla Wrubel, The Nature Company, 1973; Christel DeHaan, Resort Condominiums International, 1974; Lane Nemeth, Discovery Toys, 1978; Oprah Winfrey, Harpo Entertainment Group, 1985.

Pp. 25–26: Packard states his views in James C. Collins and Jerry I. Porras, *Built to Last: Successful Habits of Visionary Companies*, p. 56.

Pp. 30–32: On Phyllis Jordan, see Emilie Griffin, *The Reflective Executive: A Spirituality of Business and Enterprise*, pp. 112–113.

P. 35: Logan Pearsall Smith's observation can be found in Robert Andrews, *The Concise Columbia Dictionary of Quotations*, p. 276.

P. 38: On "How Christianity Changed Political Economy," see *Imprimis* (Hillsdale College) (May 1995) and *Crisis* (February 1995): 4–7.

P. 40: The poet is Gerard Manley Hopkins, the poem "That Nature Is a Heraclitean Fire and of the Comfort of the Resurrection," in *Poems and Prose*, p. 66.

Chapter Two
LITTLE-KNOWN FACTS ABOUT BUSINESS

P. 41: Meir Tamari's discussion of Judaism and commerce can be found in his *"With All Your Possessions": Jewish Ethics and Economic Life*, p. 29. Abdul Rauf is the author of *A Muslim's Reflections on Democratic Capitalism*, p. 19.

P. 42: Sources: *Statistical Abstract of the United States 1994*; Rolf Anderson, *Atlas of the American Economy: An Illustrated Guide to Industries and Trends*; and *Historical Statistics of the United States*.

P. 43: The question on church attendance was worded: "About how often do you attend religious services—every week, once or twice a month, a few times a year, or never?" The poll was conducted by Smith College's Center for the Study of Social and Political Change, directed by Stanley Rothman. Along with Robert and Linda Lichter, Rothman also published *The Media Elite: America's New Powerbrokers*, the first systematic study of the beliefs and attitudes of those working in the U.S. media.

P. 45: Paterno's most recent book is *Paterno: By the Book*.

For the numbers of Americans attending church or synagogue on a weekly basis, I have used George Gallup, Jr.'s recent "Religion in America," *Public Response* (October/November 1995): 4. For the largest television audiences, see *The World Almanac 1995*, p. 311.

P. 46: On *Commercium et Pax*: The great French philosopher Baron de Montesquieu noted in 1748 that "commerce is a cure for the most destructive prejudices; for it is almost a general rule, that wherever we find agreeable manners, there commerce flourishes; and that wherever there is commerce, there we meet with agreeable manners. . . . Peace is the natural effect of trade. Two nations who traffic with each other become mutually dependent; for it one has an interest in buying, the other has an interest in selling; and thus their unity is founded on their mutual necessities." *The Spirit of the Laws*, p. 316.

P. 46: On St. John Chrysostom's (347–407) understanding of commerce, see Joseph Cardinal Hoeffner, "The World Economy in the Light of Catholic Social Teaching," *Ordo Socialis* (May 1987): 26–27.

Pp. 47–48: I was led to reflect on my pipe by Leonard Read's famous 1958 essay, "I Pencil," reprinted in Hillsdale College's monthly *Imprimis* (June 1992).

P. 48: For Yeats and Bernanos, see Yeats's poem, "A Dialogue of Self and Soul," in *The Collected Poems of W. B. Yeats*, p. 232, and Bernanos's *Diary of a Country Priest*, p. 298.

P. 50: The pope's argument on moral absolutes is powerfully expressed and deserves to quoted at length:

> *When it is a matter of the moral norms prohibiting intrinsic evil, there are no privileges or exceptions for anyone.* It makes no difference whether one is master of the world or the "poorest of the poor" on the face of the earth. Before the demands of morality we are all absolutely equal.

Veritatis Splendor (The Splendor of Truth), no. 95.

Pp. 52–53: For Tocqueville's analysis of the effects of democracy on high ideals, see *Democracy in America,* pp. 257–258:

> In free countries, where everyone is more or less called on to give his opinion about affairs of state, and in democratic republics, where there is a constant mingling of public with private life and where the sovereign is approachable from every side, to raise one's voice being enough to attract his attention, one finds many more people seeking to gamble on his weaknesses and live off his passions than would be found under absolute monarchies. It is not that men are naturally worse there than elsewhere, but the temptation is greater and offered to more men at the same time. Consequently there is a much more general lowering of standards.

Péguy wrote of *mystique* and *politique* in his famous essay, "Politics and Mysticism," contained in *Basic Verities: Prose and Poetry*, pp. 72–77.

Chapter Three
A MORALLY SERIOUS CALLING

P. 54: Frick's famous retort to Carnegie is repeated in John Steele Gordon's "Tell Mr. Carnegie I'll Meet Him in Hell," *Audacity* (Summer 1995): 34.

P. 55: On the "social question," see Hannah Arendt, *On Revolution*, p. 15:

> The social question began to play a revolutionary role only when, in the modern age and not before, men began to doubt that poverty is inherent in the human condition, to doubt that the distinction between the few, who through circumstances or strength or fraud had succeeded in liberating themselves from the shackles of poverty, and the laboring poverty-stricken multitude was inevitable and eternal. This doubt, or rather the conviction that life on earth might be blessed with abundance instead of being cursed by scarcity, was pre-revolutionary and American in origin; it grew directly out of the American colonial experience.

For her fascinating analysis of the "social question," see chapter 2, pp. 53–110.

P. 58: Hughes and Tucker are quoted in Joseph Frazier Wall, *Andrew Carnegie*, pp. 809–815.

Pp. 61–62: On the Homestead Steel strike, see ibid., pp. 537–582, and William Serrin, *Homestead: The Glory and Tragedy of an American Steel Town*. Two other serious evils for which I gravely fault Carnegie are his insistence on a twelve-hour workday for laborers (rather than eight, which his superintendent begged him to institute) and his arrogantly expressed insistence on seven-day work weeks (i.e., work on Sunday).

P. 64: The lingering metaphysics of socialist thought were thought by the great French political scientist Raymond Aron to constitute a "Marxist vulgate." See his *In Defense of Decadent Europe*.

On greed, the distinguished former president of the American Political Science Association, James Q. Wilson, summarizes Max Weber's views as follows:

> All economic systems rest on greed, but capitalism, because it depends on profit, is the one that disciplines greed. In the process of imposing that discipline, capitalism . . . encourages civility, trust, self-command, and cosmopolitanism by first making these traits useful and then making them habitual.

"Capitalism and Morality," *Public Interest*, no. 121 (Fall 1995): 50. For Max Weber's own discussion, see *The Protestant Ethic and the Spirit of Capitalism*, p. 17:

> It should be taught in the kindergarten of cultural history that this naive idea of capitalism must be given up once and for all. Unlimited greed for gain is not in the least identical with capitalism, and is still less its spirit.

See also pp. 56–59.

P. 65: Many of David Hume's historical essays can be found in *Essays: Moral, Political, and Literary*. See in particular "Of Commerce," pp. 253–267.

On the role of intellect in devising the division of labor, see

Adam Smith's famous example of the pin-maker, *An Inquiry into the Nature and Causes of the Wealth of Nations*, 1:14–15.

P. 67: The Adam Smith quotations can be found in his classic work of moral philosophy, *The Theory of Moral Sentiments*, pp. 306–307. For a superb study of Smith's contribution to social theory, see Jerry Z. Muller's recent book, *Adam Smith in His Time and Ours: Designing the Decent Society*.

P. 68: For figures on illegitimacy, see Daniel Patrick Moynihan, "The Great Transformation," *The American Enterprise*, January/February 1995, pp. 38–41.

P. 72: Excerpts from Carnegie's *Triumphant Democracy* (which Carnegie would always consider his magnum opus) can be found in Joseph Frazier Wall, ed., *The Andrew Carnegie Reader*, pp. 207–220.

Herbert Spencer's most famous work was *The Man Versus the State*, originally published in 1884.

P. 74: Frick's latest biographer is Samuel A. Schreiner (*Henry Clay Frick: The Gospel of Greed*).

P. 75: For a fascinating short profile of Henry Clay Frick, see "Tell Mr. Carnegie I'll Meet Him in Hell" by John Steele Gordon, *Audacity* (Summer 1995): 34–45.

Josephson is quoted by Samuel A. Schreiner in *Henry Clay Frick: The Gospel of Greed*, p. x.

Chapter Four
FOR THE POOR AND FOR DEMOCRACY

P. 78: Guy Sorman's discussion of development and democracy is drawn from *The New Wealth of Nations*, p. 197.

P. 79: In *The Federalist* No. 10, James Madison rejected "pure democracy" and its violent dreams of perfect equality, while favoring the nonutopian American republic, based on common sense:

> A pure democracy, by which I mean a society consisting of a small number of citizens, who assemble and administer the government in person, can admit of no cure for the mischiefs of faction. . . . Hence it is that such democracies have ever been spectacles of turbulence and contention; have ever been found incompatible with personal security or the rights of property; and have in general been as short in their lives as they have been violent in their deaths. *Theoretic politicians, who have patronized this species of government, have erroneously supposed that by reducing mankind to a perfect equality in their political rights, they would at the same time be perfectly equalized and assimilated in their possessions, their opinions, and their passions.*
>
> A republic, by which I mean a government in which the scheme of representation takes place, opens a different prospect and promises the cure for which we are seeking. [Italics added.]

P. 80: For Max Weber, see *The Protestant Ethic and the Spirit of Capitalism*; for R. H. Tawney, see *Religion and the Rise of Capitalism*; for Karl Marx, see "Manifesto of the Communist Party," in Karl Marx and Frederick Engels, *Selected Works*, pp. 39–40.

P. 81: Representative works on the "new thing" represented by capitalism include F. A. Hayek's *The Fatal Conceit*, Israel Kirzner's *Discovery and the Capitalist Process*, and Joseph Schumpeter's *Capitalism, Socialism, and Democracy*.

P. 83: For the full stories behind J. R. Simplot and Thomas Fatjo, see George Gilder's *Recapturing the Spirit of Enterprise*, chapter 14, "The Rise of Micron," and chapter 15, "The Dynamics of Entrepreneurship."

P. 84: The phrase "built to last" is borrowed from the title of the book by James C. Collins and Jerry I. Porras.

P. 85: For Peter Berger's analysis of social democracy as a form of democratic capitalism, see *The Capitalist Revolution*, pp. 21–22.

P. 85: Concerning the necessary relationship of capitalism to democracy, Peter Berger summarizes the empirical evidence as follows: "All democracies are capitalist; no democracy is socialist; many capitalist societies are not democracies." Ibid., p. 76.

P. 90: The epigraph from Montesquieu can be found in *The Spirit of the Laws*, p. 316.

P. 90: With regard to the corrosive effects of envy, see James Madison, in *The Federalist* No. 10:

> The most common and durable source of factions has been the various and unequal distribution of property. Those who hold and those who are without property have ever formed distinct interests in society. Those who are creditors, and those who are debtors, fall under a like discrimination. A landed interest, a manufacturing interest, a mercantile interest, a moneyed interest, with many lesser interests, grow up of necessity in civilized nations, and divide them into different classes, actuated by different sentiments and views. The regulation of those various and interfering interests forms *the principal task* of modern legislation, and involves the spirit of party and faction in *the necessary operations* of government. . . . The apportionment of taxes on the various descriptions of property is an act which seems to require the most exact impartiality; yet there is, perhaps, no legislative act in which greater opportunity and temptation are given to a predominant party to trample on the rules of justice. [Italics added.]

P. 91: Alexis de Tocqueville was struck by America's freedom from envy:

> Why is it that in America, the land par excellence of democracy, no one makes the outcry against property in general that often echoes through Europe? Is there any need to explain? It is because there are no proletarians in America. Everyone, having some possession to defend, recognizes the right to property in principle.

Democracy in America, p. 238.

P. 93: James Madison remarked on the role of original sin in human affairs in *The Federalist* No. 51:

But what is government itself but the greatest of all reflections on human nature? If men were angels, no government would be necessary. If angels were to govern men, neither external nor internal controls on government would be necessary. In framing a government which is to be administered by men over men, the great difficulty lies in this: you must first enable the government to control the governed; and in the next place oblige it to control itself. A dependence on the people is, no doubt, the primary control on the government; but experience has taught mankind the necessity of auxiliary precautions.

Pp. 93–94: Irving Kristol's analysis of capitalism and its promises is from *Two Cheers for Capitalism*, p. 257.

P. 95: On "moral ecology," see my Templeton address, "Awakening from Nihilism," *First Things* (August/September 1994): 18–22, and *The Catholic Ethic and the Spirit of Capitalism*, pp. 215–220, 221–237. See also Pope John Paul II, *Centesimus Annus*, no. 50.

Chapter Five
VIRTUE IN THE MODERN CITY

P. 96: For Paul Johnson's views on capitalism, consult his essay, "Is There a Moral Basis for Capitalism," in *Democracy and Mediating Structures*, ed. Michael Novak, pp. 49–58, and "The Capitalist Commandments: Ten Ways for Businessmen to Promote Social Justice," *Crisis* (November 1989): 10–16.

P. 98: Aristotle builds up the concept of virtue step by step, inviting us to reflect on our own experience quite carefully. His first, tentative definition of any man's virtue is "the disposition that renders him a good man and also will cause him to perform his function [as a man] well." Later, he sharpens this to a fuller definition, each term of which he has taken care to build up slowly: "Virtue is (1) a habit of mind, (2) determining the choice of actions and emotions, (3) consisting essentially in the observance of the mean (4) relative to us, this being determined (5) by the following principle: *As the man of practical wisdom would determine it.*" *Nichomachean Ethics*, 2.6

1106b 36–1107a2 (Loeb translation, slightly modified). Note the flexibility added by characteristic 5. Later in the *Ethics*, Aristotle suggests a model "man of practical wisdom": "Hence men like Pericles are deemed to possess practical wisdom because they possess a faculty of discerning when things are good for themselves and for mankind; and that is our conception of an expert in domestic economy or political science." Ibid., 6.5 1140b 8–11.

P. 102: For a superb discussion of the Christian understanding of conscience, see Eric D'Arcy, *Conscience and Its Right to Freedom*. On the will, see Brian O'Shaughnessy, *The Will*.

Aristotle understood well the link between virtue and the emotions: "Habits are the formed states of character in virtue of which we are well or ill disposed in respect of the emotions." *Nicomachean Ethics*, 2.5. 1105b 26.

P. 103: Hamilton discusses reflection and choice in *The Federalist* No.1.

P. 108: Aristotle presented the relation between ethics, other branches of knowledge, and politics in the following way:

> The most authoritative of the sciences . . . is manifestly the science of politics; for it is this that ordains which of the sciences are to exist in states, and what branches of knowledge the different classes of the citizens are to learn, and up to what point; and we observe that even the most highly esteemed of the faculties, such as strategy, domestic economy, oratory, are subordinate to the political science. Inasmuch then as the rest of the sciences are employed by this one, and as it moreover lays down laws as to what people shall do and what things they shall refrain from doing, the end of this science must include the ends of all the others. Therefore, the good of man must be the end of the science of politics.

Ibid., 1.2. 1094a 27-1094b 12.

P. 110: For a long time the great exception to the philosophical neglect of virtue in the contemporary academic world has been Alasdair MacIntyre, in *After Virtue* and *Whose Justice? Which Rationality?* Of late, however, reinforcements have arrived in Gertrude Himmelfarb's *The Demoralization of Society* and William Bennett's *The Book of Virtues* and *The Moral Compass*.

P. 115: British social democrats who praise the prosaic virtues of sacrifice, community, patriotism, and duty are David Selbourne in *The Principle of Duty* and Norman Dennis and George Erdos in *Families Without Fatherhood*.

P. 116: The Nobel Prize economist is James Buchanan, and the question was posed in conversation with the author.

Chapter Six
THREE CARDINAL VIRTUES OF BUSINESS

P. 117: John Paul II *Centesimus Annus*, no. 32.

P. 119: Drucker's observation is from his book *Landmarks of Tomorrow*, p. 180.

P. 120: The limitations of Max Weber's conception of the ethic of capitalism are discussed in my *The Spirit of Democratic Capitalism* and *The Catholic Ethic and the Spirit of Capitalism*.

P. 120: The most developed treatment of the creative habit of enterprise can be found in Israel Kirzner's *Discovery and the Capitalist Process*.

P. 122: The quotations from Pope John Paul II over the course of this chapter are drawn from his 1991 encyclical, *Centesimus Annus* ("The Hundredth Year"). The implications of this encyclical have been explored by my friend Richard John Neuhaus, *Doing Well and Doing Good*.

Pp. 122–123: On man as the "ultimate resource," Simon writes:

The major constraint upon the human capacity to enjoy unlimited minerals, energy, and other raw materials at acceptable prices is knowledge. And the source of knowledge is the human mind. Ultimately, then, the key constraint is human imagination acting together with educated skills. This is why an increase of human beings, along with causing an additional consumption of resources, constitutes a crucial addition to the stock of natural resources.

The Ultimate Resource, p. 222. Richard John Neuhaus advanced this argument even earlier than Simon in his book *In Defense of People*.

P. 123: The Club of Rome's report of 1972, *Limits to Growth*, which predicted the exhaustion of natural resources in the near future, is criticized in Julian L. Simon's book *The Ultimate Resource*, pp. 286–288.

P. 124: Whitehead discusses the link of Judaism, Christianity and modern science in *Science and the Modern World*, pp. 12–13.

P. 129: For Stephen Covey's use of this anecdote, see *The Seven Habits of Highly Effective People*, p. 33.

P. 132: The text of Thomas Jefferson's First Inaugural is accessible in the Library of America's edition of his *Writings*, pp. 492–496.

Chapter Seven
SEVEN PLUS SEVEN CORPORATE RESPONSIBILITIES

P. 134: Roberto C. Goizueta made his comments in an address at Yale University, October 27, 1992.

P. 135: Erving Goffman's idea of "total institutions" can be found in his classic sociological study, *Asylums: Essays on the Social Situation of Mental Patients and Other Inmates*.

P. 136: In order to protect the right of authors and inventors to the fruit of their ideas, Article I, section 8 of the Constitution of the

United States of America affirmed "The Congress shall have Power to . . . promote the Progress of Science and useful Arts, by securing for limited times to authors and inventors the exclusive right to their respective writings and discoveries."

Abraham Lincoln's comment can be found in the Library of America's collection of his *Speeches and Writings*, 1859–1865: "The patent system changed this; secured to the inventor, for a limited time, the exclusive use of his invention; and thereby added the fuel of *interest* to the fire of *genius*, in the discovery and production of new and useful things" (p. 11).

Alexis de Tocqueville's observation of the American knack for forming associations is also worth quoting:

> Americans of all ages, all stations in life, and all types of dispositions are forever forming associations. There are not only commercial and industrial associations in which all take part, but others of a thousand different types—religious, moral, serious, futile, very general and very limited, immensely large and very minute. Americans combine to give fetes, found seminaries, build churches, distribute books, and send missionaries to the antipodes. Hospitals, prisons, and schools take shape in that way. Finally, if they want to proclaim a truth or propagate some feeling by the encouragement of a great example, they form an association. In every case, at the head of any new undertaking, where in France you would find the government or in England some territorial magnate, in the United States you are sure to find an association.

Democracy in America, p. 513.

P. 138: Montesquieu is quoted in *The Spirit of the Laws*, p. 366.

Pp. 140–141: The long quotation from Milton Friedman is drawn from his book, *Capitalism and Freedom*.

P. 142: On the obligation of creating new wealth, few others have been as clear-minded as Peter F. Drucker:

> Just as it is nonsense to say that economic life is possible without profit, it is nonsense to believe that there could be any other yardstick for the success or failure of an economic action but profitabil-

ity. Of course, it is always necessary for society to go in for a good many unprofitable activities in the social interest. But all such activities which are undertaken in spite of their economic unprofitablility must be paid for out of the profits of some other branch of economic activity; otherwise, the total economy shrinks. Profitability is simply another word for economic rationality. And what other rationality could there be to measure economic activity but economic rationality?

Concept of the Corporation, p. 193. Drucker, like Pope John Paul II, refers to profit as a "yardstick" and "indication."

On Adam Smith's idea of "universal opulence," consult *An Inquiry into the Nature and Causes of the Wealth of Nations*, p. 22 and passim, and Jerry Z. Muller's *Adam Smith in His Time and Ours: Designing the Decent Society*, pp. 63–76.

P 144: On "man's principal resource is man himself," see Pope John Paul II, *Centesimus Annus*, no. 32.

P. 145: Romano Guardini's discussion of the culture-forming dimension of religious faith is found in his book, *The Church and the Catholic and The Spirit of Liturgy*.

P. 146: For Ellen Marram's comments on her experience in business, see Marguerite Rigoglioso, "A Thirst for Challenge," *Harvard Business School Bulletin* (October 1995): 66–67.

P. 147: On the "New Class," consult *The New Class*, edited by B. Bruce-Briggs, or, more briefly, my discussion in *The American Vision: An Essay on the Future of Democratic Capitalism*. For recent antics, see Peter Berger's illuminating essay, "Furtive Smokers: And What They Tell Us About America," *Commentary* (June 1994): 21–26.

P. 148: Friedrich Hayek's argument on the incoherence of the term *social justice* can be found in his book, *The Mirage of Social Justice* (part 2 of his trilogy, *Law, Legislation, and Liberty*), pp. 62–100. For a succinct presentation of Hayek's position, see John Gray, "What Hayek Taught Communists, He Can Now Teach Us,"

Crisis (September 1990): 30–32. My own critique of Hayek can be found in *The Catholic Ethic and the Spirit of Capitalism*, pp. 62–88.

P. 150: Figures on volunteerism are drawn from a 1995 study published by the Independent Sector, "Giving and Volunteering in the United States: Findings from a National Survey."

P. 153: For the grim details on television's portrayal of businessmen, see Michael Medved's *Hollywood vs. America*, pp. 220–222.

For the Bristol-Myers and Tylenol crises, see James C. Collins and Jerry I. Porras, *Built to Last: Successful Habits of Visionary Companies*, pp. 59–61.

P. 155: Johnson & Johnson's handling of the potential risks of skin cancer from its Baby Oil product is described in *A Virtuous Life in Business: Stories of Courage and Integrity in the Corporate World*, ed. Oliver F. Williams and John W. Houck, pp. 132–133.

Chapter Eight
BUSINESS AND HUMAN RIGHTS

P. 160: For Professor Debora L. Spar's discussion of multinationals and human rights, see "Accidental Ambassadors: Multinational Corporations and Human Rights," *Harvard Business School Bulletin* (October 1995): 39–40.

P. 161: Harry Wu returned to China in 1995 for more investigative work, was imprisoned, and only after a major diplomatic tussle was sent back to the United States. Earlier, he served nineteen years in Chinese jails for dissident behavior. His book on his experiences in China, written with Carolyn Wakeman, is *Bitter Winds: A Memoir of My Years in China's Gulag*.

P. 164: For a superb collection of essays examining the thought of Adam Smith, Frances Hutcheson, Adam Ferguson, and other thinkers of what has been called the Scottish Enlightenment, see

Wealth and Virtue: The Shaping of Political Economy in the Scottish Enlightenment, edited by Istvan Hont and Michael Ignatieff.

P. 166: The epigraph, and other quotes from former Unocal Chairman and CEO Richard J. Stegemeier in this chapter, are taken from his book *Straight Talk: The Future of Energy in the Global Economy*, pp. 162–163.

Michael Oakeshott's distinction between civil and enterprise associations can be found in his classic *On Human Conduct*.

P. 171: Unocal's "statement of principles" was provided by the corporation.

P. 173: For a general assessment of the status of human rights in the post–cold war context, see George Weigel, "Are Human Rights Universal?" *Commentary* (February 1995): 41–45.

Chapter Nine
MAKING THINGS BETTER

P. 176: The passage from Alexis de Tocqueville is from *Democracy in America*, p. 485.

P. 179: The OECD's "Quarterly Labour Force Statistics," no. 3 (1995), shows the combined labor force of Denmark, Norway, Sweden, and Switzerland to be almost 12.9 million. According to calculations made by the Manhattan Institute, the total number of legal immigrants to America during the period from 1951 to 1990 was 17.7 million. See their 1994 study, "Strangers at Our Gate: Immigration in the 1990s."

P. 179: The figures on health care costs at General Motors were supplied by GM.

P. 181: On the *Forbes* health care plan, see the editorial by Malcolm S. Forbes, Jr., "How Forbes Curbed Spiraling Health

Care Costs," *Forbes* (January 18, 1995): 25. See also Rachel Wildavsky, "Here's Health-Care Reform That Works," *Reader's Digest* (October 1993).

P. 183: Rocco Buttiglione made this remark at a talk in Rome on July 24, 1995.

P. 185: Concerning the decline of the family throughout the Western world, the literature is copious. Apart from titles mentioned earlier, see David Blankenhorn, *Fatherless America*, and Patricia Morgan, *Farewell to the Family?*

On the plight of the homeless, see Myron Magnet, *The Dream and the Nightmare*.

P. 186: For the shift away from the state toward civil society as the locus for solving social problems, see *To Empower People*, by Peter L. Berger and Richard John Neuhaus, the twentieth-anniversary edition (1996). I referred to this turn as the "civil society project" in *The Catholic Ethic and the Spirit of Capitalism*, pp. 176–194. In *What Comes Next: The End of Big Government and the New Paradigm Ahead*, James P. Pinkerton advances a related argument.

Pp. 186–187: In an interview with *Hemispheres* (August 1995): 21–24, Alfred Whittaker encapsulates the ideal guiding his practical work: "Opportunity International is based on the concept that underdeveloped nations can make economic progress if they can get entrepreneurs to start small businesses and hire local people to work for them." For a theoretical statement, see my *This Hemisphere of Liberty: A Philosophy of the Americas*, pp. 49–62.

Pp. 187–188: Opportunity International has, for instance, given loans in the Dominican Republic (to a woman so she could purchase a plastic cooler to sell frozen fruit pops); Ghana (for an enlargement of a bakery owned by a woman who was then able to hire forty additional workers); the Philippines (to a dozen men starting a tricycle-taxi service); and many other locales. These small loans can make an enormous difference in the lives—and nations—of those who receive them.

Chapter Ten
GIVING IT ALL AWAY

P. 190: Brian O'Connell's comments on the philanthropic spirit both here and later in this chapter appeared in Robert Payton et al., *Philanthropy: Four Views*, p. 37.

Pp. 190–191: Andrew Carnegie's note to himself can be found in *The Andrew Carnegie Reader*, edited by Joseph Frazier Wall, p. 41.

P. 191: For the full text of "Wealth" see ibid., pp. 129–154.

P. 194: On Carnegie's views about philanthropy, see *Andrew Carnegie* by Joseph Frazier Wall, pp. 795–827. For an overview of various ethical questions surrounding philanthropy, see *Philanthropy: Four Views*, a symposium of the Social Philosophy and Policy Center.

Pp. 199–200: Merrill's views on philanthropy were conveyed in conversation.

P. 201: For an informative breakdown of the surprising patterns of funding for explicitly anticapitalist organizations on the part of various philanthropies and corporate donors, see Stuart Nolan, *Patterns of Corporate Philanthropy: Public Affairs Giving and the Forbes 250*.

Bibliography

✛

ABDUL-RAUF, MUHAMMAD. *A Muslim's Reflections on Democratic Capitalism*. Washington, D.C.: American Enterprise Institute for Public Policy Research, 1984.

ANDERSON, ROLF. *Atlas of the American Economy: An Illustrated Guide to Industries and Trends*. Washington, D.C.: Congressional Quarterly, 1994.

ANDREWS, ROBERT. *The Concise Columbia Dictionary of Quotations*. New York: Columbia University Press, 1989.

ARENDT, HANNAH. *On Revolution*. New York: Viking Press, 1965.

ARISTOTLE. *Nichomachean Ethics*. Translated by Loeb Classical Library. Cambridge: Harvard University Press, 1926.

ARON, RAYMOND. *In Defense of Decadent Europe*. Translated by S. Cox. Introduction by D. Mahoney and B. Anderson. New Brunswick, N.J.: Transaction, 1996.

BENNETT, WILLIAM J. *The Book of Virtues: A Treasury of the World's Great Moral Stories*. New York: Simon & Schuster, 1993.

————. *The Index of Leading Cultural Indicators: Facts and Figures on the State of American Society*. New York: Simon & Schuster, 1994.

————. *The Moral Compass: Stories for a Life's Journey*. New York: Simon & Schuster, 1995.

BERGER, PETER L. *The Capitalist Revolution: Fifty Propositions About Prosperity, Equality, and Liberty*. New York: Basic Books, 1986.

BERGER, PETER L., and NEUHAUS, RICHARD JOHN. *To Empower People*. 20th anniv. ed. edited by M. Novak. Washington, D.C.: AEI Press, 1996.

BERNANOS, GEORGES. *Diary of a Country Priest*. New York: Carroll & Graf, 1984.

BLANKENHORN, DAVID. *Fatherless America: Confronting Our Most Urgent Social Problem*. New York: Basic Books, 1995.

BRUCE-BRIGGS, B., ed. *The New Class*. New Brunswick, N.J.: Transaction, 1979.

COLLINS, JAMES C., and PORRAS, JERRY I. *Built to Last: Successful Habits of Visionary Companies*. New York: Harper Business, 1994.

COVEY, STEPHEN R. *The Seven Habits of Highly Effective People*. New York: Simon & Schuster, 1989.

D'ARCY, ERIC. *Conscience and Its Right to Freedom*. New York: Sheed & Ward, 1961.

DENNIS, NORMAN, and ERDOS, GEORGE. *Families Without Fatherhood*. London: IEA Press, 1993.

DRUCKER, PETER F. *Concept of the Corporation*. 2d ed. New York: New American Library, 1983.

——. *Landmarks of Tomorrow: A Report on the New "Post-Modern" World*. New York: Harper & Row, 1959.

Economic Report of the President. Prepared by the Council of Economic Advisors. Washington, D.C.: U.S. Government Printing Office, 1991.

FRIEDMAN, MILTON. *Capitalism and Freedom*. Chicago: University of Chicago Press, 1962.

GERTH, H. H., and MILLS, C. WRIGHT, trans. and eds. *From Max Weber: Essays in Sociology*. New York: Galaxy Book, 1958.

GILDER, GEORGE. *Recapturing the Spirit of Enterprise*. New edition of *The Spirit of Enterprise*. San Francisco: ICS Press, 1992.

GOFFMAN, ERVING. *Asylums: Essays on the Social Situation of Mental Patients and Other Inmates*. New York: Doubleday, 1961.

GRIFFIN, EMILIE. *The Reflective Executive: A Spirituality of Business and Enterprise*. New York: Crossroad, 1993.

GUARDINI, ROMANO. *The Church and the Catholic and the Spirit of Liberty*. Translated by A. Lane. New York: Sheed & Ward, 1935.

HAMILTON, ALEXANDER; MADISON, JAMES; and JAY, JOHN. *The Federalist Papers*. Introduction by Clinton Rossiter. New York: Mentor Book, New American Library, 1961.

HAYEK, FRIEDRICH A. *The Fatal Conceit: The Errors of Socialism*. Chicago: University of Chicago Press, 1988.

————. *The Mirage of Social Justice*. Chicago: University of Chicago Press, 1976.

HIMMELFARB, GERTRUDE. *The Demoralization of Society*. New York: Knopf, 1995.

HONT, ISTVAN, and IGNATIEFF, MICHAEL, eds. *Wealth and Virtue: The Shaping of Political Economy in the Scottish Enlightenment*. Cambridge: Cambridge University Press, 1983.

HOPKINS, GERARD MANLEY. *Poems and Prose*. Edited by W. H. Gardner. Baltimore: Penguin Books, 1963.

HUME, DAVID. *Essays: Moral, Political, and Literary*. Indianapolis, Ind.: Liberty Press, 1985.

HUSAIN, SYED SAJJAD. *A Young Muslim's Guide to Religions in the World*. Dacca: Bangladesh Institute of Islamic Thought, 1992.

JACOBS, JOSEPH J. *The Compassionate Conservative*. Lafayette, La.: Huntington House, 1995.

JEFFERSON, THOMAS. *Writings*. Notes and texts selected by Merrill D. Peterson. New York: Library of America, 1984.

KAZANTZAKIS, NIKOS. *The Last Temptation of Christ*. New York: Simon & Schuster, 1988.

KIRZNER, ISRAEL. *Discovery and the Capitalist Process*. Chicago: University of Chicago Press, 1985.

KRISTOL, IRVING. *Two Cheers for Capitalism*. New York: Basic Books, 1978.

LICHTER, S. ROBERT; ROTHMAN, STANLEY; and LICHTER, LINDA S. *The Media Elite: America's New Powerbrokers*. Bethesda, Md.: Adler & Adler, 1986.

LINCOLN, ABRAHAM. *Speeches and Writings, 1859–1865*. Edited by Don E. Fehrenbacher. New York: Library of America, 1989.

MACINTYRE, ALASDAIR. *After Virtue*. 2d ed. Notre Dame, Ind.: University of Notre Dame Press, 1981.

———. *Whose Justice? Which Rationality?* Notre Dame, Ind.: University of Notre Dame Press, 1988.

MAGNET, MYRON. *The Dream and the Nightmare: The Sixties' Legacy to the Underclass*. New York: William Morrow, 1993.

MARITAIN, JACQUES. *Reflections on America*. New York: Charles Scribner's Sons, 1958.

———. *The Range of Reason*. New York: Charles Scribner's Sons, 1952.

MARX, KARL, and ENGELS, FREDERICK. *Selected Works*. New York: International Publishers, 1968.

MEDVED, MICHAEL. *Hollywood vs. America: Popular Culture and the War on Traditional Values*. New York: HarperCollins, 1993.

MINES, SAMUEL. *Pfizer . . . an Informal History*. New York: Pfizer, 1978.

MONTESQUIEU, BARON DE. *The Spirit of the Laws*. Translated by Thomas Nugent. Introduction by Franz Neumann. New York: Macmillan, 1949.

MORGAN, PATRICIA. *Farewell to the Family?* London: IEA Press, 1995.

MULLER, JERRY Z. *Adam Smith in His Time and Ours: Designing the Decent Society*. New York: Free Press, 1993.

NAIRN, RONALD C. *Wealth of Nations in Crisis: Political, Economic, and Social Inhibitors—Enemies of Prosperity*. Houston: Bayland Publishing, 1979.

NASH, LAURA L. *Good Intentions Aside: A Manager's Guide to Solving Ethical Problems*. Cambridge: Harvard Business School Press, 1993.

NEUHAUS, RICHARD JOHN. *In Defense of People*. New York: Macmillan, 1971.

———. *Doing Well and Doing Good: The Challenge to the Christian Capitalist*. Garden City, N.Y.: Doubleday, 1992.

———. *The Naked Public Square: Religion and Democracy in America*. Grand Rapids: William B. Eerdmans Publishing Co., 1984.

NOLAN, STUART. *Patterns of Corporate Philanthropy: Public Affairs Giving and the Forbes 250*. Preface by Malcolm S. Forbes, Jr. Washington, D.C.: Capital Research Center, 1994.

NOLAN, STUART, and CONKO, GREGORY P. *Patterns of Corporate*

Philanthropy: Executive Hypocrisy. Washington, D.C.: Capital Research Center, 1993.

NORTH, DOUGLASS C. *The Economic Growth of the United States, 1790–1860*. New York: W. W. Norton, 1966.

NORTH, DOUGLASS C., and THOMAS, ROBERT PAUL. *The Rise of the Western World: A New Economic History*. Cambridge: Cambridge University Press, 1973.

NOVAK, MICHAEL. *The American Vision: An Essay on the Future of Democratic Capitalism*. Washington, D.C.: AEI Press, 1978.

———. *The Catholic Ethic and the Spirit of Capitalism*. New York: Free Press, 1993.

———. *Catholic Social Thought and Liberal Institutions: Freedom with Justice*. 2d ed. New Brunswick, N.J.: Transaction, 1989.

———. *The Spirit of Democratic Capitalism*. Lanham, Md.: Madison Books, 1981, 1991.

———. *This Hemisphere of Liberty: A Philosophy of the Americas*. Washington, D.C.: AEI Press, 1992.

———. *Toward a Theology of the Corporation*. Rev. ed. Washington, D.C.: AEI Press, 1990.

NOVAK, MICHAEL, ed. *Democracy and Mediating Structures: A Theological Inquiry*. Washington, D.C.: AEI Press, 1980.

OAKESHOTT, MICHAEL. *On Human Conduct*. Oxford: Clarendon Press, 1974.

O'SHAUGHNESSY, BRIAN. *The Will*. 2 vols. Cambridge: Cambridge University Press, 1980.

PATERNO, JOE. *Paterno: By the Book*. New York: Berkeley, 1991.

PAYTON, ROBERT; NOVAK, MICHAEL; O'CONNELL, BRIAN; and HALL, PETER DOBKIN. *Philanthropy: Four Views*. New Brunswick, N.J.: Transaction, 1988.

PECK, M. SCOTT. *A World Waiting to Be Born: Civility Rediscovered*. New York: Bantam Books, 1993.

PÉGUY, CHARLES. *Basic Verities: Prose and Poetry*. Translated by Anne Green and Julian Green. Chicago: Henry Regnery Company, 1965.

PINKERTON, JAMES P. *What Comes Next: The End of Big Government and the New Paradigm Ahead*. New York: Hyperion, 1995.

POPE JOHN PAUL II. *Centesimus Annus*. Boston: St. Paul Books & Media, 1991.

————. *Veritatis Splendor*. Boston: St. Paul Books & Media, 1994.

POULSON, BARRY W. *Economic History of the United States*. New York: Macmillan, 1981.

ROSENBERG, NATHAN, and BIRDZELL, JR., L. E. *How the West Grew Rich: The Economic Transformation of the Industrial World*. New York: Basic Books, 1986.

SCHREINER, SAMUEL A. *Henry Clay Frick: The Gospel of Greed*. New York: St. Martin, 1995.

SCHUMPETER, JOSEPH A. *Capitalism, Socialism and Democracy*. 3d ed. New York: Harper Colophon Books, 1975.

SELBOURNE, DAVID. *The Principle of Duty: An Essay on the Foundations of the Civic Order*. London: Sinclair-Stevenson, 1994.

SERRIN, WILLIAM. *Homestead: The Glory and Tragedy of an American Steel Town*. New York: Vintage Books, 1993.

SIMON, JULIAN L. *The Ultimate Resource*. Princeton, N.J.: Princeton University Press, 1981.

SMITH, ADAM. *An Inquiry into the Nature and Causes of the Wealth of Nations*. 2 vols. Indiana: Liberty Press, 1981.

————. *The Theory of Moral Sentiments*. Indianapolis, Ind.: Liberty Press, 1976.

SORMAN, GUY *The New Wealth of Nations*. Stanford, Calif.: Hoover Institution Press, 1990.

SPENCER, HERBERT. *The Man Versus the State: With Six Essays on Government, Society, and Freedom*. Indianapolis, Ind.: Liberty Press, 1982.

STEGEMEIER, RICHARD J. *Straight Talk: The Future of Energy in the Global Economy*. Los Angeles: Unocal Corporation, 1995.

STEIN, HERBERT, and FOSS, MURRAY. *An Illustrated Guide to the American Economy: A Hundred Key Issues*. Washington, D.C.: AEI Press, 1992.

TAMARI, MEIR. *"With All Your Possessions": Jewish Ethics and Economic Life*. New York: Free Press, 1987.

TAWNEY, R. H. *Religion and the Rise of Capitalism*. Gloucester, Mass.: Peter Smith, 1962.

TOCQUEVILLE, ALEXIS DE. *Democracy in America*. Translated by George Lawrence. Edited by J. P. Mayer. New York: Doubleday, 1969.

WALL, JOSEPH FRAZIER. *Andrew Carnegie*. Pittsburgh: University of Pittsburgh Press, 1970, 1989.

———. *The Andrew Carnegie Reader*. Pittsburgh: University of Pittsburgh Press, 1992.

WEBER, MAX. *The Protestant Ethic and the Spirit of Capitalism*. Translated by T. Parsons. New York: Charles Scribner's Sons, 1958.

WHITEHEAD, ALFRED NORTH. *Science and the Modern World*. New York: Free Press, 1963.

WILLIAMS, OLIVER F., and HOUCK, JOHN, eds. *The Judeo-Christian Vision and the Modern Corporation*. Notre Dame: University of Notre Dame Press, 1982.

———. *A Virtuous Life in Business: Stories of Courage and Integrity in the Corporate World*. Lanhan, Md.: Rowan & Littlefield, 1994.

WOLFE, THOMAS. *Look Homeward, Angel*. Introduction by Maxwell E. Perkins. New York: Charles Scribner's Sons, 1957.

WU, HARRY, and WAKEMAN, CAROLYN. *Bitter Winds: A Memoir of My Years in China's Gulag*. New York: Wiley, 1993.

YEATS, WILLIAM BUTLER. *The Collected Poems of W. B. Yeats*. New York: Macmillan, 1956.

Acknowledgments

✣

These reflections have been a joy to dwell on during the past few years. My wife, Karen, made dozens of suggestions—and corrections—and has long encouraged me to turn my reflections on economics in a practical direction. So, in a real sense, this book is hers in origin. Thanks, too, are due to our daughter, Jana Novak, the intrepid assistant editor of *Rising Tide,* for a final, and ruthless, proofreading.

I am particularly grateful to my longtime executive assistant Cathie Love for keeping the computer diskettes in order, amid many drafts, rearrangements, insertions and deletions; these have cumulatively produced about two linear feet of revised typescripts. My gratitude is deeper than usual because her work was interrupted by serious surgery and a difficult recovery; and because her good humor did not flag even when she felt discouraged and not quite well.

I also owe profound thanks to Brian Anderson, who read and commented on every page (including many pages now discarded), and whose ideas, suggestions, and warnings have resulted in countless improvements. He also took responsibility for executing the endnotes. Here, too, for the sake of brevity and simplicity, we cut back heavily, so that the full extent of his work is not visible.

I gladly give thanks as well to three industrious interns, Catherine I. Forbes, Alicia Therrien, and Erin Labhart, who successively helped find books and articles, wrote letters, made phone calls, and proofread. Mary Z. Hittinger did me a tremendous service in editing the penultimate draft and suggesting scores of useful corrections; she is a splendid manuscript editor, with a keen eye for detail.

Men with long business experience such as Joseph Jacobs, of Jacobs Engineering in California, and James Johnston, of the American Enterprise Institute, read parts of this book and gave me good advice about many passages—including advice to cut some of them—and good anecdotes and suggestions. To help me out along the way, David M. Abshire, James H. Billington, Jr., William C. Butcher, Joseph L. Calihan, Tully M. Friedman, Edward C. Johnson 3d, Kenneth L. Lay, Richard B. Madden, Robert Malott, Paul McCracken, Philip Merrill, Randall (Randy) Meyer, Drayton Nabers, Jr., Paul H. O'Neill, Paul Oreffice, John L. Rafuse, John W. Rowe, James P. Schadt, Wilson H. Taylor, and many others generously agreed to interviews, conversations, and/or exchanges of letters.

Gratitude is also due to the editors of publications in which earlier versions of some of the passages or chapters below first appeared; in all cases, the revisions made for this book have been substantial. Among these are the editors of *The Wall Street Journal* (for a portion of chapter 4), *Crisis* (chapters 4 and 5), the magazine *Economic Affairs* published by the Institute for Economic Affairs in London (chapter 6), and the University of Chicago Press for material from *Capitalism and Freedom* by Milton Friedman (chapter 7).

My editor, Bruce Nichols welcomed the idea of this book from the first moment he saw an outline. Both before and after reviewing three different drafts, he made creative and critical comments of great value. The copyeditor, Beverly H. Miller, swept the manuscript clean in its tiniest details, doing therein the work of God.

My gratitude to the American Enterprise Institute and its President, Christopher C. DeMuth, is immense. And so is my gratitude to George Frederick Jewett, Jr. and Richard B. Madden for the endowment of the George Frederick Jewett Chair, and to the Olin Foundation for the support of Cathie Love and Brian Anderson.

My gratitude to Pope John Paul II for his friendship and for the intellectual leadership he has provided in these last seventeen tumultuous years is even greater.

Te Deum laudamus.

Michael Novak
Washington, D.C.
December 21, 1995

Index

✦

Made in the USA
Lexington, KY
23 August 2013